For th
public library,

Comeback 2 Success

Table of Contents:

1. Introduction

In this book, my goal is to offer my own experiences, those of others living with mental health diagnoses and mental health professionals to show the overall difference a deeper understanding of mental health can make in our lives. Mental health is something that doesn't get spoken about as often as physical health. Why is that? Mental illness is often met with stigmatization rather than empathetically working to understand and support individuals with their diagnoses.

The process of coming to understand your own mental health and knowing skills to wade through the unknowns when things don't go right is daunting. I want to encourage you that you are a resilient and capable person, able to adapt to the struggles that come with having a mental illness through using the toolset I am offering you in this book.

I would like to begin by telling you my story. As a young boy, I was extroverted with a curiosity for life. In

Ferndale, Washington, where I spent the first five years of my life, my mom would pull me through the snow atop the wooden beams of my red Radio Flyer sled. We would play in the yard passing a worn-out soccer ball and climbing the mountainous playset. Our walks to the park were long and filled with joyous laughter. Nothing in life seemed to be a problem.

I vividly remember all the fun times gathered around our kitchen table playing Trouble as a kid. Life is not a carefree game; rather, is filled with many moments of trouble. My Grandma "Abuelita" taught me moments of trouble could always be overcome with the support of others. This was a lesson I held onto as I began to encounter troubles of my own. I was raised in a very conservative environment that fostered a strong spiritual faith. My Abuelita and mom taught me how to pray and how to love.

I learned how to ride a bike for the first time outside the cul-de-sac of Robyn Drive. I would watch my sister climb the steps of the school bus and impatiently await her return. Her return brought with it the promise of arts and crafts, and the daily refrain of the cookie song: "Cookie, cookie, this is what we sing to you". In times of trouble I remember these moments of bliss, young and wrapped in the sheltering arms of my small town.

Part of the safety I felt in my upbringing was the stability of going to church every Sunday. Trying to memorize the Bible verses for Bible class made me feel like I was part of something bigger than myself and my hometown. Every Sunday night we would travel to other families homes we attended church with for a weekly Bible study. My time as a youth began to take flight when we moved to the larger city of Bellingham, WA. In Bellingham I began school at Happy Valley Elementary. The teacher welcomed us all with a smile on their face and we had the chance to be kids and get to know other classmates. There were a variety of activities that we would do, like play marbles, learn to read and write and learn how to make friends. Attending school was so much fun for me because I was able to socialize and make friends.

I remember wanting to be the first in my kindergarten class to win the race around the perimeter of the playground. This is where my competitive spirit emerged. This trait has gotten me far in life. Without it, there wouldn't be a strong desire to succeed.

Through the years my family built a tradition of vacationing in Seaside, Oregon. Seaside is a small town located next to the Pacific Ocean. The town is very quiet. However, in the summertime, it is hit by groups of bustling tourists. Seaside is well known for car shows, volleyball competitions, and other conventions. I found myself enjoying everything about the town, especially the welcoming environment it provided for families. I cannot share the ease of my childhood without acknowledging that we don't get to choose our family. Sometimes childhood can be a negative experience and there is nothing that you can do to control that. Not all childhoods are filled with pleasant memories. When you are a kid, you are just trying to figure out the whole world. I was blessed with a family who loved, cared, and supported my goals and dreams. You are not alone in the troubles of life. While being in high school, I had many opportunities to grow and learn more about myself. It was a struggle trying to feel like you had to fit in with the rest of the crowd. In the midst of it all, I learned more about how to become a better me and strived to receive/give advice that was filled with happiness and joy. I Learned how to not be so judgmental towards myself. When I was in high school, I learned to overcome the obstacles of feeling judged and looked down upon because of the cliques of the "in crowd". I always felt like I was not with the "in crowd" even though I wanted to be in it. Now that I reflect on this, it is important to recognize that you don't need to be in the "in crowd" to be your happiest and best self. You are great just as you are.

My biggest self-confidence builder that supported me during middle school and high school was participating in the Rangers soccer club. That experience taught me my love and passion for the game of soccer. Releasing my energy into something that made me a better person helped me grow. There were a lot of rewards and insights to gain that helped propel me towards success in other areas and fields of life. Another important thing that I chose to do when I was in high school was to participate in various clubs such as the frisbee club and other sports that helped me to do something that pushed me outside of my comfort zone. This is something that I've valued and that helped me learn more about myself as I was navigating through being in high school. Finally, I am here to say that you can strive for better than you think. Being in high school was a test for me but it was a test that I thrived on because I finished high school with a GPA of 3.5 and with college credits under my belt.

To recap, the biggest takeaway that I got from living and being successful in high school was the commitment and dedication I spent playing soccer. This instilled in me the value of dedicating yourself to something and seeing the results that come out of your hard work. I worked on my homework every day and studied with tutors or classmates when I didn't understand a topic. I challenged myself by starting early and taking college classes through the Running Start program. I succeeded by putting all my effort into studying and trying to work on the goal which is to learn the content and pass the classes.

The running start program is valuable to any student, providing free college tuition. The program "Running Start" is specific to Washington state only. Various states might have similar programs but they go by different names. For example, in California, it is called dual enrollment. There are great ways to learn more independence and growth while at a community college. I found a lot of growth opportunities as I was with other adults studying. I encourage you to do some more research to find if there is a similar program offered in your state.

As I grew older and traveled away from the safe confines of my loving family and small town, my world was rocked like never before. Towards the end of a study abroad trip, I felt like I was living a split life. Following my return home from studying abroad in Barcelona, Spain I was diagnosed with Bipolar Disorder, at the age of 19. This was something that changed my life forever and I was in denial about it. I felt like there was no such thing as mental illness. I still struggle with accepting the diagnosis. Maybe it is because it is something that is only within your brain and body and it isn't visible like a physical disease or injury. There are thousands of natural remedies out there that can help with "curing" the illness. However, I believe that it is incurable at this moment in time. There are things that you can do to alleviate the struggle and symptoms that come with Bipolar Disorder and other mental illness diagnoses.

Flashforward to 2020, as I walk here outside in the sun in Seattle, Washington, the whole world is faced with the coronavirus plus everything that's going on around the world, it is really interesting to recognize how there is so much fear that we all have in our lives and are trying to just figure out what we can do to make do with our lives and stay happy. I want you to know that you are not alone when faced with struggles in mental health problems. I'm here to say that you can trust the process. As a result, following the steps and guidelines that are embedded in this book will give you the tools to Comeback 2 Success.

2. Academic Success and Studying Abroad

Due to the innovations of the education system and how things are progressing at universities, there are a lot of accommodations that are providing students with disabilities ways to still be successful in the classroom. There are a lot of accommodating counselors and advisors who have proven to be essential and very helpful to students with disabilities that are trying to be successful in their studies. I am basing this off of my experience as a student at Bellingham Technical College, Whatcom Community College and Western Washington University.

There are a lot of resources that you can use to become the best student and prepare you for success. When I felt discouraged in my courses, I found myself reaching out for help. I have learned that by being the biggest advocate for myself, that I can aim to get work done at the pace that works best for my capabilities. There will be times when you don't feel you can do it and that there is nobody who understands the difficulties you might be having with your studies.

A tool that I found useful was using small-group study sessions to help learn from the ideas of other students. They have been proven to spark a lot of innovation and create more of an understanding of the content which the professor lectures about at a much faster pace. When I was at Western, I learned, through group-study, an extension of the class content. It was like all the content that was learned was solidified. The beauty of trying to spend time with other classmates can spark a lot of growth.

An important concept I would like to introduce is maintaining balance in your life for your mental health. If it seems like there is too much going on, consider trying to do less, which will help you find a successful path towards graduating from college. I am still on this journey thus far.

At Bellingham Technical College I learned that there are programs that exist which can fit your needs and the level of difficulty that you are looking for. Getting a degree from a technical college is not easy. If you are thinking about going back to college, there are so many options that you have that could fit your career interests.

When someone says college, everyone seems to think of a four-year degree. I have learned that this isn't always the case. There are two-year and one-year degrees. Non-traditional education paths are able to be used to create a sustainable and profitable career. There are even certificates that take less than four years. You get to pick how to create your education path . When it comes to taking the first step, reach out to a local community college or technical college where you can get more information on the differences between the education paths they offer in comparison to a four-year degree.

I find myself enjoying life more because I am choosing to read more books. I find that reading has become more interesting for me because I have found topics on personal development and nonfiction. My perspective has changed because I understand that reading helps open your mind to new knowledge. Knowledge is power.

A book that I have read is Atomic Habits. This book helped me focus on directing attention towards habits, which helps spark growth and create a path towards success. The book Atomic Habits has been so influential for me because your actions dictate your results in life. When you choose to aim for a better way of reading and try something new, good things happen. Getting lost in a book is essential for growth.

When lack of motivation occurs to read, I start by reading just one page. After time, that one page can turn into two, and so on. Setting goals that are attainable helps spark growth and change.

Another important thing reading has done for me is allow for reflection. When you read, you have the opportunity to understand the perspective of another human being and the experiences, research and hard work that helped them create the content. I find it helpful when you are aiming to read, to start with a book that is interesting to you. When you are reading content that is essential to your growth and success, you can see that there is so much to be grateful for. The reading material can serve as a positive outlet to help gain insight on how to be happier and find some sense of enjoyment. When it comes to reading textbooks for class, they might not be the most interesting. However, I have found that talking about the reading with another classmate can help in understanding the basics of the content from the textbook.

Books help shine light on the perspectives of others, who can help to make a positive change in society. We all want to be understood. Most of us want to make a positive impact. Reading the works of others can help shed light on many different experiences and stories that are fascinating. I have found that reading nonfiction books has helped me grow and find more happiness within myself. You can do it too. I recommend using book reviews to help find a book that you think will be a good fit for your reading style. There are a lot of book review websites out there, like goodreads.com, that can help you find the right book for you. Book review sites can be used as a reference while you explore book choices that could make your life better. Also, getting recommendations from friends is a great way to find a good read.

When I was 19, I returned home from studying abroad in Barcelona, Spain. Upon my return home, I experienced a lot of confusion and discomfort. I felt different and wanted to be a different person than who I was. It was like I was in a constant battle against myself and the war wouldn't stop until I found a reason why I was feeling this way . Some of the experiences that I had while in Barcelona made me question my views on many things. The professor was teaching on anti-Christian perspectives and the history of the world. This was an awakening of my mind to other perspectives beyond what I was used to.

In my experience, I felt like I was misunderstood by the world. My brain was so confused and didn't know how to process everything that I learned once studying abroad. The only difference is that so many people have felt the same way and continued to go onto their lives while forgetting about the things that made them feel alive or passionate. Worry no more because these ideas that I have shared and what is to come will help empower you and give you direction to Comeback 2 Success.

The paragraphs below goes in depth analyzing the interview with Rich Kurtzman MA, CEO and Founder of Barcelona Study Abroad Experience. Study abroad can be a really effective way for growth despite the mental health challenges that you might be faced with. Studying abroad is a way for those with a disability to find happiness and joy regardless of what physical or mental challenges exist. There are things that are necessary for creating a successful trip.

From the perspective of someone with a mental illness or disability, there are many things that you can do to prepare yourself for such a feat. To start with, I interviewed the CEO and founder of Barcelona Study Abroad Experience, which he has led since 2009.

I asked a series of questions to go more in-depth as to how more students with disabilities can start to study abroad? The first question and answer was:

Interviewee: Rich Kurtzman, MA

Date: May 28, 2020

Time: 8:30am PST

Brandon: What is your educational background? Can you tell us a little bit about your work related expertise?

Rich: Studied Spanish and Russian in Undergrad and a little bit of Business and Psychology.

Rich: Studied Abroad in St.Petersburg, Russia.

Rich:Studied Abroad 1 Semester in Madrid, Spain.

Rich:Masters Degree in Spanish Applied Linguistics and Second Language Acquisition

Rich:Worked for Study Abroad Organization in the U.S.A. where he was recruiting.

Rich: Taught Spanish, Intercultural Communication, Internships and worked in various cultural and academic side in Barcelona

Rich: Started Barcelona SAE in 2009. Founder and CEO.

The next question and answer was:

Brandon: What are some of the ways you want the study abroad programs globally become more accessible for students with disabilities?

Rich: TODOS - The Outcomes Based Diversity Outreach Strategy. Increasing Inclusivity in study abroad and trying to help more underrepresented students go abroad and increase the training for them as well as staff, homestay families.

Brandon: When I got to interview Rich, he mentioned that Todos is a great way that they are giving a voice to those with disabilities and the minority population.

The next question and answer was more related to what study abroad programs could be doing to add value to the student who is studying abroad with disabilities. This is a big challenge that many organizations are trying to solve and create more accommodations to help give more opportunities for those with disabilities to study abroad.

Brandon: How can study abroad programs accommodate better for providing students with disabilities with an opportunity to study abroad successfully?

Rich: Letting them know that it is possible. There are resources that can be provided for you. There will be resources that can help your university. For Barcelona, mobility is the best and public transportation with more lines that are there for support. Logistically, housing is something to keep in mind. Continuous follow up and support.

Brandon: The next question focuses on what Barcelona SAE is doing to help make a change within their program and Rich gives some recommendations for those that are interested in studying abroad with a disability.

Brandon: What are your hopes as you look forward to becoming a more accessible study abroad program?

Rich: More students have the opportunity to study abroad and have a memorable experience like myself when I studied abroad in Barcelona, Spain. Having a role model to help lead a path for future study abroad students who are interested. Take the leap of faith!

Brandon: The leap of faith that you take will come with risk. Without calculated risk, there is no reward. Over the skype interview, Rich shared with me the story of a girl in a wheelchair who had the opportunity to study abroad and sink her feet in the meditteranean. This dream came true because of the accessibility that Barcelona SAE and the staff provided for this student. There are so many resources that exist out there that can help other students who have disabilities whether it be mental or physical health. It is a matter of standing up for what you want and going for it.

Brandon: What can study abroad programs improve upon with their support for students who faced culture shock? Reverse culture shock?

Rich: Preparation is the key. It is helpful for study abroad programs to have pre departure programs to help create a better transition.

Rich: And guided reflection by experts in the program to discuss what students are going through and see things from a different perspective.

Rich: Especially to be more accessible to all students, this has to come in different formats: written, verbal, conversation.

Brandon: All of this is what can help remedy the realities of culture shock and reverse culture shock. Going into a deep depression is something that is real and can have a tremendous impact on someone's life post study abroad. I say this because I experienced reverse culture shock first hand.

Brandon: Guided reflection is another key idea that Rich brought up during the conversation. The concept is simple: give other students the ability to freely open up about what they learned and how they are going to apply the experiences back at home.

Brandon: The next question talks about: What is the best advice you can give to a student with a disability who is considering studying abroad?

Rich: Talk to somebody else who has done it. Might have a similar disability. Be as prepared as you can by talking to professionals. Make sure it is the right thing. It is not the right thing for everyone. Maintain support networks from a distance.

Rich: Be prepared to not be prepared for everything.

Brandon: Be optimistic and follow your heart. The law of attraction is attracting you to what you want to become a reality.

Brandon: There is so much opportunity if you learn to apply yourself to the growth and impact that you have for your life. Gaining insight from others who have been faced with heavy depression or any other mental health struggle is a great place to start. The fear of loneliness will come to light only if you let it stay with you permanently.

Rich: I shared my bit of guidance and advice about optimism and following your heart. Your instincts will attract you to where you want to go in life. The fact that you want to study abroad is the first start. The next thing to think about is how you should "be prepared to not be prepared for everything".

Brandon: The next question talks about how there are some problems that are trying to be answered better to accommodate study abroad opportunities for those that are faced with a mental health condition. This next question is proposed to unveil some of the things that are holding back so many programs from finding the success to open their programs to accept those with mental health struggles. During the conversation with Rich, he mentioned some of the pivotal industry changing solutions that can help remedy the problems and create results that will encourage students with mental health problems to pursue their passion for studying abroad and traveling.

What are some big problems that the study abroad programs are still facing related to mental health and disabilities?

Rich: "The number of students with disabilities are growing very quickly. More instances of anxiety and depression. Just means that we as a study abroad program need to be more prepared. Not everyone is a licensed doctor and understands the medication. Resources for professional help would be of great benefit. Being prepared for the increase of students studying abroad with disabilities"

Brandon: There is so much to be gained from a study abroad trip. If the study abroad programs give more funding for counselors and other licensed doctors to provide aid for students with mental health struggles, there can be a big change in the study abroad community,

Brandon: The next question that I posed to Rich was if he had anything else he wanted to share with you… "Anything else you would like to share?"

Rich: "We have had some incredible and inspiring students in the past who have been in wheelchairs, deaf, with cerebral palsy, mobility challenges, mental health issues, and all sorts and I am so proud of them for taking the challenge to come abroad, when it is challenging for anyone to begin with, but with extra challenges, it's that much harder. Some of my best memories are working with the students who "gave us more work" logistically but the reward is priceless."

Brandon: Overall, the reason I decided to interview Rich was because of the impact and passion that I have for studying abroad. There is so much that you can learn about yourself and find growth through travel. You can be so happy and content with traveling and learning different cultures. With that being said, when you have a mental illness or any other health struggle, I get that it can be hard to travel and live out something that you believe you don't think you can do. With that being said, I encourage you to look at your options and see what could work for you in your academic journey. Below is the Barcelona Reflection when I returned to Bellingham back in 2015.

12/16/2015

"Coming Back from Barcelona has been one of the hardest things I have ever done emotionally. I was hit with culture shock hard. I felt like my whole life was just beginning without everything that I was raised and expected to be. Every day I grew to be a very independent person that would go out and do things that made me happy. I had nobody checking in with me and seeing where I was going. Nobody asked me where I went. I felt like I could be whatever type of person I wanted to be. My Spanish was improving every day that I was there because of how many friends I had that were locals. I have the potential to get even better because of my Spanish level. Every day, my peers and host family challenged me by letting me grow as a person. I felt like I had nobody telling me what to do. No influences except whatever my heart desired.

In Morocco, I was amazed at how simple of a life that my host family had. I was so moved by how giving and loving they were towards me. They would give and expect nothing in return. I felt a love that I will never forget. Their lifestyles were so much more simple. They did not make a lot of money, yet they were still happy with what they had. They lived their lives everyday in a more basic way. Sometimes the more basic is where you can focus on the things that really matter.

Guillem, my friend, showed me the life of a Catalan student who was working hard, going to college and still making time for friends like me. He explained to me that even relationships that last for 4 years don't always turn out great.

My feelings on Barcelona as a whole are this city has helped me open my mind tremendously. I was so naive and innocent coming into Barcelona. My first opinion on the trip was that my family would be so loving and want to do a lot of stuff with me. Reality hit me when I got there because the family was not comfortable with doing anything else besides the meals and talking. This turned out to be the best thing for me because I learned that not everyone has a life that is all smiles. Life is rough. I am figuring out how to accept this. Now, I was able to see many different types of people that exist in this world. My world expanded tremendously out of the little city of Bellingham in which I was born and raised.

Another very important trait I got to experience was patience. Not everyone will do what you want when you want. I had my regular routine in Bellingham before I left. Events or plans rarely changed. I was in total control. In Barcelona, people were more slow paced and relaxed with everything. This taught me to be patient and know that something will not happen when I want it to happen.

When I am in Barcelona I feel like I can be whatever type of person that makes me happy. People let them be and give them their own choice to develop their own views and thoughts on life. This might be very outspoken in comparison to their eyes. I feel like

Barcelona, France and Morocco have changed me by the way I see the world."

Now that I am without a job and struggling to find the freedom that I was granted in Barcelona, I am feeling down. Coming back to the U.S. has shown me the type of person I can become. I was offered a job in Real Estate. I turned it down because I had too much going on in my life mentally.

If I go back to Europe and Barcelona, I think I would become a better person. While I was over in Barcelona, I never had any homesickness like many of my peers did. I found this really strange. I think this was because many of the students did not make such close connections with the locals like I did. In detail, my family shows love by asking me about everything that I am doing. I value my happiness.

My time volunteering at La Ecola de la Sagrada Familia gave me a perspective on teaching that I would have never imagined. I learned a little bit about what it takes to be a teacher. Since I am fluent in English and my dream has always been to be fluent in Spanish, I am considering pursuing a career in teaching English. Coming back to the U.S., I was given another opportunity to explore my teaching abilities. I gave a lesson on how to drive a stick-shift to my friend. I felt calm, happy and relaxed when I taught. When he was successful, it gave me true happiness.

Now, I am faced with a big decision. I am starting to look at my options for finishing school in Barcelona, at Western Washington University or at The University of Washington. What now? As time goes on, my views and choices might change. I created a lifelong relationship with my host family and friends in Barcelona. At this point, I could see myself living a happy and more fulfilling life in Barcelona, or at least somewhere in Europe. My goals right now are to work as much as I can, save up, find a school that will accept my transfer degree and move back to Barcelona.

Heck, I know that when I was just 19, I felt like I was fearless and ready to take on the world. That is the way everyone should be in order to reach their biggest goals and wildest dreams. Unfortunately, it wasn't long after when I suddenly hit a wall and life threw a gut punch at me. The reality is that once I worked hard and earned the trip to Barcelona, I grew up and learned more about myself and about life. The trials and tribulations that you have or will face help shape you as a person and are a blessing or a curse, depending on how you see it. Life doesn't always go the way we want it to go.

Learning languages with a mental health diagnosis

Learning languages can be difficult but rewarding once you get over the hard work that must be put into it. I wanted to share with you how I didn't let depression stop me from doing what I love. As I mentioned earlier, my return from the study abroad trip in Barcelona, Spain made me feel lost and depressed. I decided to try something different that was outside of my comfort zone. That was taking a Chinese class. This was hard enough juggling two other classes that both required a rigorous amount of time to study. I found myself waking up at 5:30am to study just to do so poorly on the quizzes. My mental health was lacking. The lesson learned is that you need to have a good balance between life and studies. During this troubling time, I wasn't sleeping and found myself struggling to find my place in the world.

The Chinese class helped me grow and learn a lot about Chinese culture. All the while, I wasn't sleeping much. My depression seemed to be getting worse and worse. I finished the class with a C- and felt content because of how hard I worked to earn this, while handling the internal and external circumstances.

The point I am trying to get at is that we all have an ability to stand up or be a self advocate when we are feeling low. If you have been faced with a mental health diagnosis, letting it defeat you when you want to try something new, like learning a new language, will only be cheating and depriving yourself of your potential. Many times I felt like giving up and dropping the class. But the support that I got from my classmates and tutors are what helped me push on and feel happier, regarding my language abilities.

You as a person get to choose who you want to be. Learning a language helps you learn more about yourself and the world around you. When faced with a mental health diagnosis, things can feel low and gloomy. Trying something new and pushing your comfort zone can be very rewarding if you put the effort into it and take the risk.

When life got me down and I was depressed, I met my friend, Ming, who was from China. He is bilingual, fluent in Chinese and English. He was very helpful and encouraged me to learn Chinese. Also, his perspective was unique on mental health as he had faced similar circumstances that I went through.

We are so similar as humans and can learn a lot about someone based on their different cultural backgrounds. You have the innate ability to learn a new language even if you were diagnosed with something like Bipolar or any other mental illness.

Your work ethic sets you apart from your mental illness. While studying Chinese, I found myself spending a large amount of time with tutors and classmates to learn and understand the concepts. Don't get me wrong though, I did start learning the language in an advanced level class. Being committed to learning a language can help your brain think in different ways. The path that your life takes can be inspired tremendously by what you learn in the classroom.

As Americans, we serve as a strong example of people who stand up for what we need. We can help inspire others to follow the steps to cultivating a happy and healthy lifestyle while living with a mental illness. My challenge for you is to take a look online and discover something that could help you learn a language, which could make you happier and a more wholesome individual. I use the Mango app on my iPhone where I can brush up on practically any language.

FOR FACULTIES AT STUDY ABROAD PROGRAMS:

From a student's perspective, the faculty at universities would be more well equipped if they had mental health counselors. This is important because when studying abroad, you are thrown into a place that is unfamiliar. Students with a mental health diagnosis are more susceptible to a relapse or crisis when there is a large number of unknowns. When I was studying abroad, there was a helpline that you could call. This is a valuable service that could help students who are homesick and might be experiencing depression or loneliness.

When structuring a study abroad program, there are some steps to consider when hiring staff. It would be beneficial to have a staff that has gone through a certification class on mental health.

When studying abroad, students are in a foreign place where the language that is spoken is not always their native tongue. As a result, it is harder to communicate with the local community. This is important to think about because if you aren't able to communicate in another language, it can be isolating and feel like you are in a place where you feel misunderstood.

Following the HUG method can really help a faculty member to embrace students and meet them where they are at. I developed the HUG method to help faculty members in order to better equip them to help a student under a lot of pressure and mental discomfort. Firstly, the H stands for" helping" the student, being open to hearing them out and what they are experiencing. U means trying to "understand" them and meet them where they are at. Lastly, "gain insight" on what can be done to help resolve the crisis or relapse and develop a strategy together, that will help the faculty to become more educated in mental health and to help solve the student's problem. Taking the next step towards a comprehensive mental health program can take your school's program to the next level and attract more students living with mental illnesses to study at your institution.

Traveling with a mental illness

On another note, travel can present additional challenges to someone living with a mental illness because of the fast pace required by traveling and changing time zones which can be drastic, depending on the distance that you are traveling. Implementing proper techniques into your life can help you prepare for a successful trip wherever your destination might be. Preparing for a trip requires mental and physical proactive planning since your body is about to undergo a temporary change of lifestyle.

Traveling by plane opens doors for opportunities in your life. There is nobody that should be in your way besides yourself as long as you are able to take your mental illness seriously and focus on a happy and healthy lifestyle. The best advice I can give is to give yourself plenty of time to sleep before and after the trip. Proper sleep as you transition to your destination will help you prepare for a fun and rewarding time abroad or domestic destination.

When traveling abroad you will experience cultural and language changes. The farther distance you travel will increase the culture and language changes and create less stability. Getting outside of a stable environment will create room for a relapse. I strongly recommend that you don't travel abroad if you just got released from the hospital or are in the middle of a crisis. I wanted to go back to Barcelona while I was in the hospital. My doctor and nurses explained to me that it was not the ideal time to be traveling, as I needed to rest and recover from being in the psychiatric ward. Deciding when to travel is entirely up to you. Listening attentively to the ideas and recommendations of mental health professionals is a great place to start as you plan your next trip. The opinions of family and friends is another valuable place where you can receive advice.

When you are making plans for a trip, I would recommend that you consult with your mental health team to get advice on how to follow a plan that will help you have a successful trip. Furthermore, start planning on backup strategies and know that you can have support in the event of a crisis. It is a good idea to be prepared for the best and worst case scenario. Taking action and being educated on your mental health status is a key factor in a fulfilling trip. This is so important to do because you will feel more confident in living, knowing that you are aware of yourself and your limits.

One Positive experience I had while traveling was the chance to learn more about myself from a different lens. On the other hand, there were times when I felt overwhelmed and had to resort to being alone or sleeping in later. However, I firmly believe that you should try to get up out of bed early so you can be energized and ready for the day as it comes. Our biggest mistake will be not actively planning for a trip in a way that can help you in your personal growth and make you a happier person. I want to encourage you to start small and work your way step by step, seeking your dreams and accomplishing your goals when it comes to traveling, studying abroad and/or vacationing.

3. Know Yourself: Understanding Your Diagnosis

Life put my head under water and I had to learn how to pick myself up from the bottom of the sea and swim towards my dreams in the midst of a storm. How does someone like myself go when there is so much pain and sadness after being diagnosed with something like Bipolar disorder? The truth is, I really live my life to the fullest and accept where I am at. The goal is to take all of it one step at a time.

I am going to be honest with you. I challenge this diagnosis every day, but I have learned to accept that I am in a place where I didn't think I would be, because so many people said I would fail and need an excessive amount of support for the rest of my life.

Most of the time we create our own problems. I, for the most part, seemed to be my worst enemy. I was stubborn. It wasn't until I really fell and started to realize that I had a problem that I felt I needed external help. I have learned through all of my mistakes and failures, that I can comeback 2 success and be successful in whatever area of life that I set my mind on.

Being diagnosed with bipolar disorder is like having an invisible cloud over your head that is waiting to erupt into a storm. The goal is to make sure that clouds only produce rain naturally and that the storms are avoided. We all go through mental health struggles and nobody is immune to them. Even if you don't have a mental health struggle, you still will face many emotions in life. Being prepared to process them at all costs is what separates intelligence from ignorance. Living life when I was on the soccer pitch with my teammates as we went on to win the Washington State 2A soccer championships felt like a breeze compared to what I had to endure during the early stages of receiving my diagnosis. It is interesting to see how life changes when your mindset changes after you get some experience under your belt. Going through the ups and downs of life and forging a life for myself has been so rewarding. Mistakes are a part of life but they don't fully define me as a person.

This chapter aims to educate you on various diagnoses to help you on your journey. Even if you aren't diagnosed with a mental illness, things like depression and anxiety are still things that need to be handled and managed properly. Web MD gives a good general synopsis of what you need to manage and maintain when faced with a mental health diagnosis. Web MD states, "Millions of Americans live with various types of mental illness and mental health problems, such as social anxiety, obsessive compulsive disorder, drug addiction, and personality disorders. Treatment options include medication and psychotherapy." (Goldberg "Types of Mental Illness"). It's simple, this statistic showcases how important this topic really is. It is all about gaining awareness of yourself and your lifestyle.

Furthermore, I want to break down various mental health diagnoses and go more in depth so that you can be well informed about what to expect if you, a loved one, or another member of your community is experiencing a diagnosis.

To start with, anxiety disorders are very prevalent amongst Americans. We seem to not be aware of them because while physical injuries can be visible, mental illnesses are not. According to webMD, "People with anxiety disorders respond to certain objects or situations with fear and dread, as well as with physical signs of anxiety or panic, such as a rapid heartbeat and sweating. An anxiety disorder is diagnosed if the person's response is not appropriate for the situation, if the person cannot control the response, or if the anxiety interferes with normal functioning. Anxiety disorders include <u>generalized anxiety disorder</u>, panic disorder, <u>social anxiety disorder</u>, and specific <u>phobias</u>" (Goldberg "Types of Mental Illness"). There is a distinct difference between anxiety disorders and other mental health disorders. Being diagnosed with bipolar, I have experienced a litany of similar traits. However, like anyone in life, it is normal to have feelings of distress. If you haven't, you are lying to yourself. There have been certain scenarios while in the hospital where I had to take actions that would keep me in a stable mindset. An example is when I stayed in my room to avoid any type of conflict with hospital staff or other patients. I remained secluded on one side of the hospital room to isolate myself from the rest of the patients. The hospital really changed my views on how it is to be in a place like the psych ward, which is a place nobody wants to end up in.

In continuation with anxiety disorders, if you are dealing with this and have similar symptoms, I encourage you to take the first, and sometimes hardest step, to confide in someone about your feelings. Sometimes the feelings and rush of experiences that happen in life overwhelms us and leaves us with so many questions. The best piece of advice I can give, specifically to individuals who are unsure if they have an anxiety disorder or not, is to not be afraid to reach out to a support network. The support network could be your family or best friend. The doctors don't really get involved unless you let them and open up to them. When it comes to taking any type of medication, **I am not a licensed psychiatrist** so I do not have the ability to give you advice on whether or not you should be taking any kind of medication.

The next type of mental illness that I will cover is the mood disorder. This is what I have and experience every day. The definition that Web MD uses is, "These disorders, also called affective disorders, involve persistent feelings of sadness or periods of feeling overly happy, or fluctuations from extreme happiness to extreme sadness. The most common mood disorders are depression, bipolar disorder, and cyclothymic disorder." (WebMD). These symptoms are hard to deal with because they make life more difficult than it needs to be. Without determination, persistence and commitment to care for yourself, you aren't setting yourself up for success. The hardest steps are reaching out for help, being humble enough to listen and make wise choices based on what the mental health professionals offer you when you are struggling. Following this, you can make your own decision as to whether you want to listen to what they have to say or go your own way.

The bipolar mood disorder is something that is well known for its relativity to make someone angry all of the time. This isn't my truth with the disorder. It is more so, that it is hard to adjust to abrupt life experiences and finding balance can be a struggle. There are certain triggers that can cause a manic episode to occur out-of-nowhere. I can relate to this, as when I was returning home from studying abroad in Barcelona, Spain I fell into a deep depression and couldn't seem to get out of it. My parents practically forced me into the hospital with the help of the local police department. I was already struggling with a lack of sleep and now it seemed worse because it felt like there was no escape from the mental health department until the doctors said I was better. The feeling of not knowing when I would leave such a dark and scary place like in the psych ward really started to wear on me. As a result, I had to find out what to do to change my way of living so that I can be in a better position to set myself up for success both in the short and long term.

Being diagnosed with bipolar has really taken a toll on my life and I would definitely consider it as being something that forced me to take two steps back in life. I suffered many losses going through the hospital. What did I learn? Life is too short to not to try to overcome your mental health struggles. You should Humble yourself to take a leap of faith and put yourself out there when you need it the most. This advice is based on my own experiences that have led me down the road to success.

I want to elaborate more on understanding your diagnosis. This could look like simply doing some online research. However, the harder and more rewarding path is sitting down in a group setting and hearing other people explain how they are focusing on their mental health recovery. Life can be complicated. A mental health struggle, like depression, can make it almost unbearable at times. Taking the journey of life one step at a time is where you will find rewards.

Another example of how you can become more familiar with your diagnosis, is doing things the hard way. I always seemed to go the hard route and as a result, I ended up in some very dark places. When I took the hard route in understanding my diagnosis, life took me to the hospital, a halfway house, a mental health program in Atlanta and had me living in hotel rooms. Life seemed to be a never-ending cycle of relapses. It was only until I realized that I needed to stop avoiding my diagnosis, like I have done for a long period of my life, that I finally started to face it head on. This was hard to do as it is harder to look at your problems from within than it is to blame something or someone else, especially given the stigma that surrounds a mental health diagnosis. This is something to keep in mind when determining where to start. **The hardest part of the journey is to accept your diagnosis and understanding it more is the first step.** You get to choose how you accept your diagnosis and move forward towards your goals. I encourage you to try out something new that will help you release your tension and fears from yourself. Establishing a friend group that helps support you and helps you understand more of who you are and how to work in tandem with your diagnosis will give you even more power to shoot for the stars.

The opinions of others on your mental health are only important if they are coming from people who you are close with. Listening to outsiders who aren't aware of your experiences and struggles is not helpful in discovering your truest self. The diagnosis that you were given by a mental health professional is justified based on the evaluation that they gave you.

If, for some reason, you feel that there is a difference of opinion regarding your diagnosis, the best way to go about making a change is to reach out to a loved one who is wise and you can trust. Challenging your beliefs is important in fully accepting your diagnosis. By following up regularly with a mental health professional, you can learn more about your diagnosis and the symptoms. Life becomes easier when you manage your actions and are able to see if they align with the diagnosis. This can be further explored by doing reality checks. This is when you take a step back, recognize your actions and reflect on how you are feeling. As a result, you will get a better sense of understanding as to how you feel at a certain time and how to react to that specific emotion.

The diagnosis that you were given is justified based on your experiences, behaviors and life struggles. If you have struggled with mental health problems, a good way to engage in a healthy and open discussion is to attend different mental health therapy groups that encourage opinions to be shared on diagnosis and growth. I found so many rewards and received positive feedback from attending different groups that helped make a positive impact on my life. For example, I attended the NAMI group on mental health. I got to listen to stories on how people are living their life. Many of them are trying to find success and are continuing to strive for their dreams and goals.

As for the rest of society, I have found that, in my experience, there are people who will be naysayers and don't agree with how you are living and treating the diagnosis. It was hard to accept but sticking to my gut and true colors has helped me significantly overcome the struggles of dealing with the judgement and opinions of others that come with a diagnosis like Bipolar Disorder.

Challenging your beliefs about your diagnosis can be a good thing, depending on how you look at it. This will only help you strengthen your ability to accept where you are at in life.

You have a choice as to how you react to society and how people react to your actions. Only you get to decide how you will receive proper care to overcome the mental health struggles. Some ideas for how to avoid conflict based on differences in opinion include:

1. Get support from your mental health team

2. Cultivate positive relationships with people who are open-minded and receptive toward your mental health struggles

3. Continue to persevere through the struggles and finding hope that you will see better days for time to come

4. Accept where you are at and take steps to get to where you want to go

Separating yourself from the crowd and engaging with a personal, in-depth strategy that gets you results and focuses on health habits is the key to managing this. From my experience, I have found that relying on a firm structure of friends and family has proven time and time again to help me become more informed about Bipolar and how I can be in constant control over this mental health condition.

The next topic that I want to bring up, is the critical idea of self-acceptance of your diagnosis. Depending on what that is, you have the choice to stand up for what you believe in, even when it is hard to swallow. The acceptance is sometimes the hardest part of the battle. For me, this is something that I still struggle with at the age of 24. I have been diagnosed for over five years now. I want to make it clear that when I was diagnosed with Bipolar Disorder, I struggled for years denying that I had this disorder. Even in the present day, the mainstream approach and view on bipolar isn't very accepting. Individuals with mental health challenges are similar in that most individuals don't view you as equal. The biggest takeaway that I want to give to you is to not fight it. Do whatever it takes for you to accept where you are at mentally and make good decisions to be proactive and ensure that you are living a happy and healthy lifestyle.

Nobody is going to change the way you are and make you who you want to be, no matter how much you want it or pay. Personal growth comes from within yourself. Don't give up. This is the hardest thing people have to do because they are too scared of what it might entail. For me, my failures were my biggest successes because it got me to where I am today. It is something to be thankful for because without my failures, I wouldn't have seen my biggest successes and dreams come true.

For anyone dealing with any type of mental illness, there are multiple paths you can take to find your true value and worth. If you recognize this, you can choose to succeed even if you have fallen and don't know where to go. Acceptance, just like anything, takes steps when it seems that there is no route. Your key that you need is inside of you.

The next topic that I wanted to introduce to you is an in depth analysis on case managers and psychiatrists:

Case Managers: They are there for your moral support and want to see you succeed. I like to think of them as a life coach. They usually have a B.A. in a social science program. They are required to develop a care plan with you that covers many questions and what to do to prevent an accident or relapse in symptoms.

Your case manager is a resource that you can use to bounce ideas off. They are supposed to be supportive and help you get to where you want to go. What is a typical session like? They last 30 minutes to an hour. They are meant for following up on areas that can be improved upon.

This leads me to doctors and psychiatrists. They are there to support you with medications, which are supposed to keep life in balance so that life can be lived at an optimal level. Positive results are what we all want to have.

Friends as support: Your feelings are valuable. Before talking about what your friends can do to support you in a mental health struggle, I recommend that you learn how to find the right friends. My definition of a good friend is someone who you can trust and who cares about you. Genuine friendship doesn't cost a dime. Being with each other is what makes life better and that is what I define as real friendship.

So, with that being said, it is vital to find friends who you can confide in and will give you supportive advice and constructive criticism. Your friends can give you suggestions on what you can do to get your life back on track. You are who you hang out with. I know for me; it was easier to reach out to friends about my mental health struggles than with my family. The way I was brought up encourages me to resist getting help with mental health. I had no idea that I would become diagnosed with Bipolar Disorder. Finding the right friends is something that is noteworthy. In my experience, I reached out to too many people. Some of them turned out to be the wrong friends that didn't help me to grow in a healthy way. Sometimes making the mistakes of knowing what a bad friendship is, helps you find where good friendships lie. Overall, don't make the same mistakes as someone else. Learn from them and see what you can do to stay on track.

4. Learning how to live well: Hospitalizations, halfway homes and self-help programs

I was faced with a lot of difficulties in the psychiatric department at the hospital. The first night I was woken up by a man that was dressed in a white apron and scrubs with a big security guard badge. I felt like I was a star and a prisoner at the same time. I felt like a star changing the world with my story as I was escorted down the halls to the psych ward. At the same time, I felt like a prisoner because I didn't know when I was going to go home and leave that place that was so unfamiliar and contained. This experience was my definition of hitting rock bottom. I cried myself to sleep that night.

I woke up the same way I went to sleep-balling my eyes out in front of the sign of people who had a mental illness and were famous. I told myself that I would be up there with them one day because I had a vision that nobody could take away from me. My greatest challenge was accepting my diagnosis.

Similarly, life in the halfway house was hard. I had to overcome the fears and stigmas that existed in my life. This experience really made me grow up quick at the age of 20. I felt so lonely and like there was nobody around to pick me up but myself. I had to learn to walk my own path in this world.

Spending the time inside the halfway house helped me put my life into perspective and realize that even though I am in a dark and scary place, I knew how to keep going and strive for a better day. There were multiple times when I couldn't take it inside the halfway house. I would pay for an Uber because I had no car at the time. The Uber would take me to a hotel (with the minimal amount of money I had) for the night so I could escape from the struggles and fears of living with a group of people who are severely mentally ill. I felt like a king at The Four Points Sheraton on Lakeway Drive in Bellingham, Washington. Many people would have broken down, made a bad decision or given up due to the circumstances that I was facing but I did not. I remained resilient and continued to forge a path towards enrichment and success.

Nobody has walked the path that I walked when crying myself to sleep as I pondered why life has put me into a place that is so dark. Going through many hospitalizations as well as a stay in a halfway house taught me to stand back up and overcome the struggles by relying on friends and family who want to see me succeed. The pride and desire to be successful attracted me to Skyland Trail in Atlanta, Georgia for 3 months.

In 2017, I was discharged and had to live in a boarding home with severely mentally ill people who could hardly function and take care of themselves. This was for five weeks. However, I learned how to be self-sustaining during this time period. All the tears that I shed in that boarding home made me stronger. The biggest takeaway that I want to share with you is how important it is to be accepting of yourself and recognize the feelings you are having. Be patient with yourself, have kindness and self-compassion for the hard parts of life you are trying to embrace. Connecting back to the boarding home, I kept my head down and persevered despite not having a method of transportation and having minimal support from friends. I felt severe fear and felt like I was being pushed outside of my comfort zone. I was thrown into the ocean. It is important to recognize that there are a lot of people who have similar symptoms and don't know where to start but have overcome their obstacles. The reason for which I am writing this is to help you open your eyes and look at yourself from within, to see who you really are and discover your inner passion.

Agate Heights, A part of Lake Whatcom Center in Bellingham, WA was a terrifying experience. I, however, didn't give up. All the tears and pain I had to endure made me stronger and gave me the will to write this book. Without the experiences, I would not be the man I am today.

The Agate Heights house was very scary because I had to accept that I had to live through this for over a month right after being hospitalized in the mental health department. Through this experience, I realized thatI need to rely on mental health professionals for support to overcome the struggles that exist in life when faced with Bipolar Disorder.

The positive part about being inside the Agate Heights Facility is that I learned more about myself. The amount of social isolation and separation helped me move forward in my journey.

The multiple hospitalizations helped me grow and recognize that the isolation is temporary. The time spent by myself was what I needed to learn how to accept myself. The sadness and tears are parts of the journey that help us learn how to be better people. You get to choose how you live your life. The support from others and recognizing that you need to make a change is pivotal to improving your mental health and recognizing that we need each other to be happy.

Crying myself to sleep as I pondered why life put me into a place that was so dark was something I had to learn to accept. This helped me learn to stand up and overcome the struggles by relying on friends and family who want to see me succeed. Even though I wanted to stay in Bellingham, WA to work at Fred Meyer, I am glad I made the decision to go to Skyland Trail.

As I go more into depth about Agate Heights Mental health facility, I suggest that if you are in a dark and lonely place, my faith in God has helped me overcome the mental warfare that I experienced in life during those difficult days.

Another positive aspect about being inside this facility is that I learned more about myself. The month of social isolation and separation from society for a month is what helped me move forward in my journey so it can be made more authentic. The multiple hospitalizations helped spark growth within myself and accept that the isolation was temporary. The time spent by myself is what I needed to learn how to be accepted by myself. The tears and sadness that are part of the journey can help us as we learn how to be better human beings. I am here to say that in life, you get to choose how you live. The support from others and recognizing that you need to make a change is pivotal for improving your mental health and recognizing that we need each other to be happy.

Finally, the time in the Agate Heights facility was transformative because I learned how to be happy just being me. Regardless of the negative emotions, I learned that I could still rely on music and myself. As I approached the end of my time in the Agate Heights Facility, I learned that if I kept trying, I could eventually see success and the goals that I wanted.

Adjusting to life with a mental health diagnosis is hard. If you feel that you are having a hard time talking with someone about your diagnosis and want to see a change in your life, try counseling. Speaking with a psychologist or Licensed Mental Health Counselor (LMHC) helped me navigate my journey of life and bounce ideas off of people who are mental health professionals and could give me advice on how to live a happy and healthy life as I worked through my struggles.

Your life is too important to give up on yourself and shut the lights off. Based on the failures and struggles that I have persevered through, I am here to say that you can do the same. There are so many struggles and life lessons that I can proudly say that I learned to overcome because I didn't give up.

Giving up can be easy when you feel so alone. The first night I was in the hospital was the loneliest I have ever felt in my life. The cold metal bed was my only companion that night. I longed for the days of my childhood once again, surrounded by the ones I love.

Getting out of your comfort zone is what you can do to find the growth and reap the rewards of facing your giants. Living in a major city like Seattle and in Los Angeles County, I find myself being around a lot of different people who have different walks of life. I bring this up because you are special for who you are no matter what upbringing you came from. The world is big and you can make a big imprint on it.

When I was in the mental health department, I conversed with many individuals who were all walking towards recovery in the best way for them. Being inside the mental health department (One Central) was not an easy thing to do. I didn't make it easy on myself because

I was resistant and in denial towards the treatment that the hospital staff was trying to give me.

Recognizing what you have at your feet and determining what it takes to keep your life in balance helped me to accept the treatment plan hospital staff created for me. My definition of diagnosis management is understanding and implementing what you need to do in order to live a happy and healthy lifestyle. I always focus on keeping track of my mental health with each choice that I make to improve and enrich my life. Each day I ask myself questions such as: Am I giving myself enough time to rest? When I am feeling great, how do I maintain this lifestyle? When I am not feeling great, what do I need to do to improve my mental state? These are all critical questions that need to be addressed when finding your truth for what makes your boat float.

When dealing with a mental health problem, things can quickly go from bad to worse. Following these steps can help save lives and prevent people living with a mental illness from giving up.

Step 1: Self awareness- In my past experiences with going through a crisis, I found it helpful to try and recognize where I am at and stay planted to understand the way I am feeling and the symptoms that are occurring in my life at the moment.

Step 2: Confide in someone you trust and who can help give you some feedback on the way you are feeling in your life at the moment. This could be a friend or family member. No matter what, locate someone as a method of relieving the unknown and negative feelings or symptoms that you are experiencing. Just talking to someone that's in your corner can be a game changer. Another example of confiding in someone may look like reaching out to a mental health professional. Nobody wants to be in the hospital. For some (like myself), that's what it took to make a difference in life and carve my own path. It was like I was running and running from myself until finally, I hit a wall. The crisis ended with me staying in the hospital for over a month. This was a dramatic and mentally exhausting experience that has shaped my life in many ways. As mentioned earlier, my biggest recommendation that I can give to you is to focus on confiding in someone you trust who is educated and knowledgeable in the background of mental health. A list of the professionals includes a doctor, psychiatrist, case manager, therapist, mental health program and fellow peer who has the same or similar diagnosis. Just by talking with someone who can empathize with you and your feelings helps alleviate the uncertainty and negative feelings occur when in a crisis.

Step 3: Take initiative to take charge of your life. When in a crisis, re-establish stability in your life by focusing on one thing at a time. This looks like taking responsibility for your actions. You can learn to manage your condition and be stable by focusing on yourself and finding peace from within by taking responsibility for your life and caring for yourself. Don't let the stigma of other people deter you from finding self-peace. Don't over complicate your life when life can get hectic and crazy for everyone. Taking charge of your life is like taking the bull (your life) and taming it. Learn to tame your inner self and control your actions by putting yourself in a place where you can begin to retake control of your life. When I get overwhelmed with life, I take one big and deep breath to recalibrate and help press the reset button on my mind.

Step 4: Accept change: This is very important when you are going through a crisis because change is never easy for anyone. We as humans are always experiencing this. Value the importance of accepting when changes are needed in your life to overcome the circumstances and situation that you are facing in your life at the moment. Being diagnosed with Bipolar at the age of 19, I didn't want to change. I've had to work on myself and understand my diagnosis better to develop a sense of connection with my condition to create success and stability in my life. This is relevant for anyone who has never experienced depression in their life before and is going through it for the first time. It is critical that you accept where you are at and let go of the mental barriers that we all have blocking us away from our truest selves.

Step 5: Be bigger than your mental illness:

Establishing a routine when you get out of the hospital is critical for success. This is something that will vary depending on how long a person has been inside the hospital. In my experience, the best way to focus on your recovery from the hospital is to give yourself a comfortable bed. Sleep is one of the most important things that will help you on your journey to success and to overcome the hard change of pace that real life presents when outside of a controlled environment like the hospital.

The steps to a successful routine are balance and consistency. It all starts with your mindset including how you start your day to execute what you have planned to accomplish. My typical day out of the hospital was pretty lowkey because of how long and mentally exhausting the hospital was. I started my day by sleeping in a lot. When it is hard to sleep, listening to some soft music helps to pass the time when you are restless. Your choice of music can help set the mood and tone for you in the present moment.

Next, find some hobbies that help keep you busy and do something that makes you happy. Reading a good book is always a great place to start. Doing something with substance will always help you personally develop yourself while the struggle of acclimating back into a normal routine can be a challenge. Some other examples of good and healthy activities could be as simple as cleaning your living space. This is very rewarding because you are taking responsibility for your life and can have more peace of mind because you are taking control of your life in the best way that you can.

Find a program that helps give you aid in your endeavors as a support team. This looks like meeting up to connect with friends to find innovative ways to get your life back in order. Hospital transitions programs have other past clients who have gone through similar walks in the mental health industry. The peers help with ideas on how to better improve the client that has recently been discharged from the hospital. As a result, they have a lot of experience and knowledge that can be shared with you when trying to Comeback 2 Success.

Certified peer counselors play a pivotal role in advocating for the clients of the hospital who are faced with a mental health diagnosis or anywhere in between. They provide a transformative approach for helping you with your diagnosis because of their experience as a recovering and self-sustaining peer with a mental illness. There is a lot of value and knowledge that can be transmitted from these roles because of how seasoned they are with living in the hospital first-hand and experiencing the ups and downs of the psychiatric ward.

I encourage you to think of mental health professionals as part of your team who want to help you get to where you want to go in your life. They are in your corner helping you navigate your health to a happy and healthy level. Being unhappy, depressed and all over the place doesn't have to be that way. As an individual with Bipolar Disorder, I am very aware that I can think of the mental health professionals that I work with as part of my life in a way that is helping me accomplish my goals. Think of them as part of your support team and want to see you at your best. You are in the driver's seat of your life and can work intuitively with the mental health professionals to better develop yourself into the person you want to be.

Further, a case manager is someone who you work with to hit your daily, weekly, monthly, etc. objectives. For some, it might be hard to even make your bed every day or to take care of yourself. Case manager's are like life coaches that help people who have significant mental health problems. Case managers are usually easier to talk to than the doctor because they have more time on their hands than the doctor does. Case managers are there for your mental health support and have a plethora of ways to help send you on your way to success. Use them as a resource and a way to bounce ideas off someone who can relate to you and understands your perspective.

Nurses are also a pivotal part in ensuring that your needs are met with a mental health diagnosis. Nurses have experience with handling medication. Nurses can help with administering medication to the patients. Some clients rely heavily on nurses to provide patients with the medication that is needed to maintain a balanced and healthy lifestyle.

Receptionists are generally the friendliest of the hospital staff because they are there to welcome you. Of all the mental health organizations that I have been to, the receptionists always made a big impact on the first idea of how someone will like or dislike the organization.

The goals of the staff at a mental health organization are to help you succeed and achieve your goals. As a client, you are in the driver seat of your life and control how your care is directed. Typically the doctor has the knowledge and expertise to help you get a diagnosis and control what types of medications that are recommended. This is only if you need it and agree to it. Next, the case managers are a very important part of establishing care. Following this, the nurses are important because without the medication for some with a mental health diagnosis, there is no sense of success that can be achieved. The chemical imbalance might not be controlled.

Before going into the hospital, there are a lot of resources that are there to support you and overcome your obstacles. To break it down, your resources start with yourself. Then your friends, family, doctors, psychologist, therapist and case managers all follow (order varies from person to person). Also, therapists/psychologists play key roles in preventing hospitalizations. You have a choice in how you react to the emotions you are experiencing. Reaching out for help does not guarantee that things will change immediately. There will be times when you are going in the right direction but the world seems to be crashing down on you. This was me when I entered the mental health hospital at PeaceHealth.

A General Overview of the Psych Ward

The psych ward history goes way back in time to the 5th century in France and Syria. The article "An Illustrated History of the Mental Asylum" explains what the conditions were like and how through time, things are changing. However, there is still a tremendous amount of changes that needs to be made. DNews from Seeker.com says, "Most sufferers of mental disorders throughout history have not been treated as patients, but rather as prisoners" (DNews). The way that people are treated inside mental health institutions is very similar to the way things are nowadays. There are tons of psych wards and mental health institutions around the world that are experiencing a lot of horrific conditions. After doing some research, my experiences with the mental hospital seemed more laissez-faire (or hands-off) in comparison to others.

Another point that I wanted to bring up was how mental health institutions are evolving over time. Author of the Article, "An illustrated History of the Mental Asylum" breaks down these concepts and shows how things are changing in the mental health industry. DNEWS states, "As patient care became a higher priority for mental health professionals as opposed to simply corralling patients into a facility to segregate them from society, what were once called lunatic asylums gave way to psychiatric hospitals" (DNEWS). The idea of being in jail just for having a mental health problem is really extreme to think about. I believe that through my experiences, the stigma really comes into play for societies who can't relate to the experiences that individuals have gone through when they have been a part of a mental health institution for a short or long period of time. This shouldn't stop anyone with a disability from pursuing a life filled with the pursuit of happiness.

The first time that I was put in the mental health department of PeaceHealth, I was put through the ringer. I had never been so scared in my life when a large man escorted me to the psych ward and sat me down. The psych ward had a lunch room. And multiple rooms you were sometimes required to share with other people. Each person had a bathroom. That night, I cried myself to sleep and I had never felt so close to God. I prayed "God please protect me".

The typical day consisted of waking up at 8:00am or earlier. Breakfast was served at 8:30am. The morning meeting group started at 9am. At 10am there was another morning group. Morning group would look something like a group discussion about mental illness. We went through various activities discussing development, growth and overcoming the stigma about your diagnosis. There was some motivational content that the therapists walked us through with various activities. Dogs were brought in on occasion to help boost morale and give animal therapy.

Following this, lunch was served at 12:30. Once again, the food is terrible. If you have walking privileges, at 1pm you could walk around the hospital for 30 minutes or so. Other times, it took a couple of days to earn the privileges. This entirely depends on the patient and the evaluation of the doctors.

Upon return from the walk, there were afternoon group activities and snacks. The afternoon activities looked like playing Wii and focusing on improving the overall mental health of patients including myself. The environment was focused on being very therapeutic. The patients, however, can be really loud and crazy during this time. They are unbalanced and going through a lot of inner turmoil with their diagnosis. I suffered being inside the psychiatric hospital and wish I never had to go through the pain of being inside for multiple weeks on many occasions.

In the evening, we would have dinner. Then, we would have a group activity like game night. Most of them were in a lost place, like myself and had no sense of direction. In the evening time, it would be really depressing because when I didn't have visitors, I felt lonely. I noticed that it was hard to be happy in a place like this. There are a lot of patients who just need to figure out their lives and don't know who can relate with them in their life.

What is NAMI and how can they help you?

If you are diagnosed with a mental illness, NAMI is a great place to start that will help guide you on your journey in life. NAMI has locations around the United States. When I got out of the hospital, I started attending the NAMI group therapy sessions. The two hour session was spent hearing the perspective of others on mental health and how they cope with their diagnosis. This can be very effective because you are able to voice your feelings in a confidential place where you can feel welcomed and accepted for where you are at.

When I walked in, there were other people sitting down. I was welcomed by the group leaders and signed into the group. Then you were able to chat with a couple of other group members and feel like you can just have a normal and easygoing conversation. This was great and fun as it helped to normalize and destigmatize living with a mental illness.

Some of the topics discussed were on mental health and how you are working on improving this. Your habits are what got you to where you are. Another point I wanted to bring up is the fact that everyone in the group has a story. Their journey has been altered and they have had to readjust their lifestyle and life to accommodate the circumstances when faced with a mental health diagnosis.

Overcoming your problems in a setting like NAMI is a powerful place where you can expect to see changes made within yourself and others. Just like how it goes in life, you get what you put into it. As a past attendee of some of the classes, I noticed a lot of people felt comfortable sharing their goals and how they are constantly aiming to improve themselves and find some sort of inspiration to keep them on pace for their life.

Because of this, my biggest recommendation for anyone looking for a group therapy class is NAMI. The class that I went to was free. All you have to do is have a mental health diagnosis to join. This organization is transformative for many lives of individuals who have a mental health diagnosis. If you are one of those being affected by this, I encourage you to get some more information and look for a local branch to try it yourself and get the care and support needed to pursue your passion and an enriching life.

This looks very different for everyone as we all have different ways of finding balance within ourselves. Our environment sometimes is out of our control. However, we can control how we respond to the circumstances that we are faced with daily. We all need to find a place where we can feel like the rest is helping nurture our bodies and mental health.

When I was living in hotel after hotel for a couple of weeks, I found that due to the mania, it was hard being able to find rest and an environment that was stable. I was living in a temporary home that was an unhealthy living style. I was isolated from the rest of my family and friends.

Some steps you can take to focus on creating a stable environment is to find a happy place where you can let yourself go emotionally and mentally. This could be in your room, for example. As a kid, and even now, I have found that my room is like my happy place where I can find peace and tranquility where I can recharge my brain so that I can function at an optimal level and engage in the daily grind of life.

The environment that we create to have stability is crucial to the stability of our mental health. The next activity I want you to think of is the 3 places where you find your happy place that can help you cope with the depression or any negative symptoms from your condition:

Step 1. Is the environment quiet enough?

Step 2. Do you have time for yourself to be alone?

Step 3. Is there enough lighting for your brain to think and recharge?

Some of these ideas have helped me set up a prime environment that has helped me when I had a rough day at work. Stability is created through time and a commitment to oneself and your overall needs as a human to mentally recharge their batteries. It is vital for you to stay grounded and find attachment to a place where you can be uplifted from the troubles and stresses that come with life.

Also, certain activities or routines can provide you with stability. It could be going to watch a soccer match once a week where you get soaked up in the environment and it completely boosts your mood. This is something that I have discovered that helps me to be physically more stable. Every part of your body is important and giving yourself energy in all shapes and forms of it will be rewarding and uplifting for your life.

I challenge you to start looking for ways to uplift yourself and foster an environment where you can say that you are finding your happy place and feeling content with your life. The lives we live can be incredibly stressful. Creating a stable environment is like the safe place of a best friend. When you can embrace the comfort of a place where you can find peace and serenity, things change and you can start developing yourself. So, what does your ideal environment look like that will keep you stable enough to pursue your wildest dreams?

It can be hard trying to focus on your goals for your mental health and you can be very discouraged to give up on your dreams. I am here to say that you can still live a fulfilling life pursuing your passions even when you have a mental illness. It takes a lot of grit, persistence, and empathy for yourself to know your limits and understand when you can push yourself to grow.

When I got out of the hospital in Fall of 2018, I started my recovery slowly. I focused on getting lots of sleep to ensure my brain could function properly. Next, I slowly took strides in increasing my physical health activities through walks and soccer. I realized that by taking things one step at a time, created results that were astronomically rewarding.

The best part about growth is through the tough times. Learning to accept yourself and meeting yourself where you are at currently is what can get you the results that you are looking for.

In the broader overview of life, celebrating a small piece of success will help you cultivate results that will help you on your journey through life. My definition of being a go-getter with a mental illness is someone who has the power to choose how they live their life and who doesn't let their circumstances defeat them. Whenever I got discouraged (which happened a lot), I chose to buckle down, reach out to my resources that helped me grow and focus on the tangible things that needed attention and were achievable at the moment.

For example, I tried going back to school multiple times over the past 4 years since I graduated high school. From this experience I learned that you have to give yourself patience, self love and respect and trust that the work you are putting in towards self-development can be very helpful and rewarding as you start to see results.

School challenges one's ability to focus. Further, education is an investment in yourself where you can actively engage in creating a routine that gets you the results you are looking for.

On another note, some examples of focusing on your health and your goals is to encourage yourself that you can do it even if you are weak. Easier said than done right? When you are weak, you are most vulnerable to failure. Failure isn't always a bad thing because you can really learn a lot from it depending on your attitude.

Mental Health Organizations: What are they?

Mental health organizations are typically non profit organizations funded by the state they are in. Mental health organizations exist to make a difference in the mental health of individuals who have mental illnesses like bipolar disorder, schizophrenia, PTSD and many other diagnoses. They can be a very transformative place for people to come and get help. The hardest part is for the people to decide to reach out for the help. If they don't accept that they need to make a change in their life, there is a low chance that a transformative change can be made.

From my experience with mental health counselors, I can say they are professionals who are supportive and help you stay on top of your goals so that you can be happy and successful in your life. When I was struggling, for example, my faith in God helped me stay on track for where I wanted to go and what I can see my life turning into. I firmly believe that when you find Christ, you will feel more wholesome and complete. When days felt immensely hard, I realized that I have endured so much adversity.

When you feel like your back is up against a wall and your "enemy" (inner critic) is trying to see you fall, don't give up because it's on you to decide when it's your turn to rise to your potential. This takes a lot of time, energy, dedication and commitment. You must want it so bad that you are obsessed with it. When you aren't winning, you are focusing on how you can win and achieve your goals. Having a positive mindset is something that I am learning to do every day. When things are negative that are going on in your life, push forward and start looking onwards towards a bigger and brighter future. There is nobody stopping you from reaching your peak of potential besides yourself.

Money and Mental Health:

I am not a certified accountant or financial planner. I am writing this based on my experience with using my money to successfully live a happy and healthy lifestyle. What I do know is that if you work hard enough, are patient and passionate, the money will come. These fundamental steps are what will get you to where you want to go:

Step 1. Have a plan for what you want to save up for.

Keep your mind centered on the number that you are striving for. Regardless if you have a mental illness or not, you have the ability to work and save to benefit yourself and your family in the future. Hard work pays off in the end.

Step 2. Consistency is key

Whether you just started a new job, are trying to look for a job or are on your way to becoming an executive for a company, consistently showing up and being prepared will lead to success. I show up to work on time to set the tone for the day. By keeping up this good habit, I am ready to take on the challenges that come my way while on the job.

Step 3. Ask for advice

Other people who have been successful financially and have well-established savings habits are the ones who you should consult. Why trust someone's advice who hasn't done it or isn't embodying what you are wanting to become? Especially if they have concepts and ideas in the field of business that you are looking to earn income from.

Step 4. Believe in yourself

By believing that you will become a millionaire, you will manifest this goal into reality (with work and time). Setting big goals will help you aim high. If you don't hit your largest goal, you can at least say you tried and that you will hit close to it.

Step 5. Create attainable goals

Attainable goals measure what is feasible in the here and now and can get you where you want to go. Having a clear picture of what you want and understanding what it will take to get there is half the battle. The execution part of it comes next.

Step 6. Execution: work, work, work

You can't stop until you see your results. Most people start trying and once earning money gets hard, they give up. You only reach success and monetary freedom when you stay in the game. Money is the byproduct of the work that you are investing into your life and can give you freedom to do the things you love in life.

An example of using money wisely was when I worked as a car salesman and for Fred Meyer, I saved up enough money to invest in myself by paying for college classes. I then saved up enough money for my move to Seattle and Southern California. This has changed my life immensely.

Money can be used as a tool for accomplishing your goals and finding stability in your life. You can become successful and monetarily free if you are able to stay balanced and have a hard work ethic. I am continuing to support myself in Seattle and Southern California. Life is yours to live how you want to. It is a great idea to budget your income so that you have total control of what is coming in and out of your finances. The reason why I have been successful by moving to Seattle and Southern California is because I have budgeted my time and money well. I found myself focusing on the necessities and not falling into temptation for the things that I don't really need (cars, expensive clothes, non-essentials). I also limit how much I go out to eat. Instead, I focus on bringing lunch to work every day.

The bottom line is that if you don't try to balance your finances, you won't learn something from the experience and be able to make good choices with your money. And end up in debt which prohibits you from funding your passions. Money is a tool for your success and goals. Treat it like so and it can fuel your passion and get the results that you are looking for.

From my perspective, you should be investing your money into your passion: plain and simple. With these pieces of advice, I encourage you to stand up, take control of your finances and discover that you are capable of becoming financially free.

On another note, when I got out of the hospital, there were times when I didn't know where to start to find my Comeback 2 Success. There were days where I would sleep most of the day and night just to embrace the fact that I was struggling and depressed. Being bipolar comes with a wave of emotions and feelings that can make waking up in the morning difficult.

Sometime along your journey in life, you will find yourself trying to tread your own path and discover what you need to do to maintain your balance and happiness. Happiness is the key to winning in life.

Everyone must go through some type of adversity for it to last and strive for the million-dollar dreams.

Your recovery is strictly up to you to find the serenity and aspirations to overcome your obstacles. When I found myself in a dark place I had to pick myself up and keep forging onward into the unknown. Walking until you see the light of success and happiness is what it will take to get you where you want to go in life.

There will be people who try to bring you down and want to see you fall again, but there is more support than you think. It is up to you to aim for positivity and get rid of the negativity in your life. Aiming to get over the unknown and continue your walk for the light of success is where you will find contentment and happiness.

Your recovery is unique as it is catered towards your way of living life. Your recovery requires help from others. Your recovery starts from within where you will continue to find passion and strength when things get tough.

I had to give myself grace when I ended up moving to Atlanta, Georgia for 3 months and went through the Skyland trail recovery program in August of 2017. There were times when I wanted to give up.

Also, finding meaning in my life is what helped me stay focused on gaining the most knowledge and expertise that I could about myself. Having those difficult conversations with people about their journeys and struggles is what helped me gain more value and insight as to say that I wasn't alone in this battle.

My best piece of advice that I can give you when you are going through something difficult is to just keep going. When I say this I mean keep trying to live and put effort into your life. The sweat and tears that you create will be the guiding light towards the true passion and purpose why you are on this earth. Your vision for what you want to have in life might be the only thing that you have to hold onto. There is absolutely nothing that is stopping you from your success and goals in life. Dreams do come true if you are willing to put in the work.

You are not defined by your mental illness or any other condition and diagnosis. Just let it be as it is and learn how you can transform your struggle into a strength. The struggles are what make you who you are. Your ability to stay on top of your dreams and sacrifice your life for your passion is where you will find the truth that you are looking for.

If you have learned to accept failure, then you will be set. The concept of letting failure guide you and your path in life is where you will find the results you are looking for. I have found when there are times that you don't feel a place where you belong, it is up to you to get the help you need to function at your best.

You are only kidding yourself if you are choosing to neglect your mental health. I was running away from my diagnosis of Bipolar Disorder for a long time until I finally realized that I can control Bipolar and myself so that I can become the man I have always dreamed to be. There is nothing getting in the way besides yourself to do the same. I have found that the results are gained when you are embracing the struggles of life.

5. The Writing on the walls: A collection of interviews detailing mental illness diagnoses and experiences

I had the pleasure of interviewing a mental health counselor. We discussed a lot of topics concerning mental health and how important it is to have a counselor. Counselors seem to be surrounded by stigma because they are thought of as an extra hand that some people don't need. At least for me, at the age of 19, I was very reluctant to talk with someone and share how I felt as I processed my life.

Brandon: I asked the Licensed Mental Health Counselor a list of questions that he answered and gave his experiences as a counselor to formulate his answers. He has a masters degree in Clinical Psychology. The first question was "How can counseling have an impact on patients with a mental illness?"

LMHC: His response was, "At a basic level, instilling hope and empowerment and understanding the symptomology and strengths" (Licensed Mental Health Counselor).

Brandon: From a counselor's perspective, they have the ability to change lives and make an impact on the patient that is transformative. In all of the counselors that I have seen, I have learned that you get what you put into it. The counselor is there to guide you in your journey and be a navigator that helps provide you with healthy outlets that will help you engage in a healthy and happy lifestyle. The hope portion of it is very true because when faced with a mental health diagnosis, how do you have hope that overcoming the diagnosis will help guide you in your journey of life. Life is already hard enough. Adding another diagnosis to make life more complicated will only make things more of a struggle. Using your resources and being self-motivated is the key to your success in maintaining your balance and mental health.

Brandon: The next portion of their response as they instill

LMHC:"empowerment"...

Brandon: that comes from the patient as a starting point to vocalize their needs when being diagnosed with a mental illness. This empowerment that I have seen looks like empathy and meeting you as a client where you are at and providing ideas and advice for how you can stand tall and strong for your overall mental health.

Following this, the LMHC mentioned

LMHC: "Understanding the symptomology and strengths".

Brandon: This looks like understanding your symptoms a lot more so that you are well equipped to control yourself and having the knowledge to understand when something isn't going right. You as an individual have your own strengths and the counselor is able to work on your strengths to help get you to where you want to go. I recommend taking the step and trusting in a counselor to share your feelings with as they will be able to provide you with insightful information and input on what your next steps should look like in life. You have a choice on how you live your life. The counselor is there to help build you up. The end goal is perspective which is everything in life.

Brandon: Another important idea about the counselor is the fact that when finding one, it is all about finding the right one that fits. The best way I can put it is like a pair of shoes. You don't know until you try it out. The LMHC also explained his idea on how counseling can make an impact...

LMHC: "Ultimately at the root of every condition, you can develop a strength and unique perspective to practice resilience. The ultimate goal of counseling is to develop insight that allows one to ultimately treat oneself with all the necessary treatment resources available" (LMHC).

Brandon: Opening the floodgates of resources and taking action is what it all boils down to. Choosing a resource and going for it all in. Start looking at the opportunities that your counselor and other mental health professionals can give you and you will start to see a change in your life.

Question 2

Providers are a pivotal part of the recovery process for individuals who have been faced with a mental illness. There are many times when the provider is the biggest support that someone can have. They are able to help guide you in your journey.

After having a great discussion with an experienced LMHC, I learned a lot about how the providers are trying to get better to give better care to others who are struggling mentally. I asked the big question,

Brandon: "What can providers do to better improve the care that they can provide their patients?" And the response they gave me was

LMHC: "Constant learning. Lifelong learning and educating themselves constantly throughout their career. Patient focused and what the patient's strengths are. Collaboration and education" (LMHC).

Brandon: From a providers perspective, the idea of constant learning and growth is what will give mental health professionals the equipment needed to help such a large population in our community.

Brandon: Another aspect of the response that they mentioned was… LMHC: "education constantly throughout their career"…

Brandon: that really stands firm with the pillar of living life and trying to be a better provider for the client. Their perspective is really interesting as the big question is how do providers get better when they are trying to see growth and improvement in their patients. What does this look like? From a client perspective, having the experience and educational background is the fundamental of being able to effectively counsel someone and help them as they navigate their journey of life.

The counselors are a very important part of the mental health team for the client that is struggling with any kind of depression. That is why the importance of finding growth within the field of counseling, there can be breakthroughs in care and the approaches that counselors take when advising their clients.

Brandon: Another important concept is

LMHC: "collaboration and education"

Brandon: Which makes everyone better. Reaching out to others for advice to be a better you and a better counselor is where the results can be improved upon. Apply yourself like your life depended on it because you are in the driver seat of your life and career. The success of your practice relies heavily upon your willingness to collaborate and continue your growth inside your field.

Brandon: Overall, as a clinician and LMHC, you get to decide how your approach is to working with your clients. The ideas that I got from interviewing the LMHC provide you with a framework on how you could better improve your practice and see results that will last. Also, a very important Idea that I had was stressing the importance of attending classes that are aiming to improve your career as a counselor.

Brandon: From a patient perspective, just having someone to vent to is the most basic and important thing that can help aid someone in their mental health struggles. This takes us to the million-dollar question. What is the biggest problem that clients with mental illness face on a daily basis?

LMHC: "LMHC's opinion is that access to care and stigmatization and a lack of awareness of mental illness. Access to care and acceptability" (LMHC).

Brandon: When society and the community provide others with a welcoming hand to get access to mental health care, others can be impacted greatly and feel encouraged to face their problems to focus on wellness. The ability to have an open mind and provide a healthy outlet of support can impact the community tenfold.

Brandon: Stigmatization is another great point because within the American society and culture, many people choose to fight through the feelings that they are going through in an unhealthy way. Individualistically speaking, it starts with you to overcome the stigmatization that exists in the world relating to mental health. Your voice is more valuable and impactful than silence.

Brandon: Following this, lack of awareness of mental illness is something to be considered when adding value to society and creating a more sustainable lifestyle for everyone. Stigma is a great topic that I seem to fall back upon a lot. As discussed in the earlier chapters, this is a topic that is essential for our society to make a change and move forward with society's viewpoint on mental health. This is because we need each other to be happy and without the guidance and support from others, life is harder. Overcoming the stigmatization is half the battle when you have support from others who are empathetic. The lack of awareness goes in tandem with stigmatization because without the proper education that exists out there, society and the majority of the population will remain uneducated and informed. As a result, ending the stigma of mental health can be of much help to guide a community, nation and world in their objectives to help people.

Brandon: The acceptability is something that starts with one individual learning more about themselves. Then taking a step out of their shoes and putting their perspective inside the other persons. That is where the true growth can be found. Mental health is a new subject that is foreign to many people. Even for me, when I was diagnosed at 19, Bipolar and mental health was so new and foreign to me. As we look into the future, it is important to take one step at a time to focus on improving the community's mental health.

Brandon: The LMHC also went into describing what the approach is like for mental health education. They say

LMHC: "Strength based approach to overcome stigmatization... Looking for whatever the patient has in their life and character and ability to allow them to empower themselves to direct their own growth. As mental illness is viewed... grow to heal and recover from the mental illness to develop strength" (LMHC).

Brandon: This way of tackling their mental health struggles can create results that will last a lifetime for people. The idea of empowering others who are struggling to stay mentally stable can be a guide to navigating someone on a good life path. The recovery from the mental illness exhibits a lot of growth and has overall kept me on a path of success.

Youth are not exempt from dealing with mental health struggles. There are a lot of diagnoses that exist out there where the adolescents are struggling with a mental health diagnosis or symptoms. In fact, like I said earlier, I was 19 when I was first diagnosed. That is why from a community perspective the best way to treat this problem is to focus on developing a large support system. At an early age, it is crucial to have support which will help kids who are faced with the same reality and change of pace in life.

More importantly, the best response that LMHC offered was to the question, "who is the best support system that can help improve the lives of the adolescent with a mental health diagnosis or imbalance. Their response was "Family is the greatest source of support. For a family, recommending psychoeducation, family support, family systems therapy and community support" (LMHC). After learning this, it is important to recognize the impact that the family and community can make to inspire and create a positive change. This impact is only started when you put yourself out there and try to be empathetic about the struggles of what someone is experiencing in their life.

The next question that I posed to the LMHC was "What are your biggest recommendations for someone who is interested in seeing a counselor?" His response was "Start with referrals from people that you know personally. Start with your doctor, family members and friends that might be a good fit" (LMHC). This is a great way to learn more about yourself and the opportunities are endless when it comes to finding yourself and really getting the chance to find yourself again. Taking the first step is always the hardest part. Another idea that can help put you in the right direction is to go into the first counselor appointment with someone you trust and who you feel can be very transparent with you. The first couple of visits might be hard and awkward. You are taking the first step that is pivotal for your life so that you can see yourself succeed and blossom into the person you want to become.

The referrals that you get from peers, family members and online can be a good way to navigate your journey of life as you engage in a healthy way of growing as a person. Your family and friends know you the most and can help guide you in your journey to overcome the stigma of seeing a counselor and sharing your thoughts with someone who wants to support you.

It is very interesting how my mindset has changed about counselors as I was once very against it and didn't want to see a counselor for a long time. Things got worse until I eventually ended up in the hospital. Moral of the story, sometimes taking a step back and humbling yourself to share what's on your mind is what you need to do before you can take two steps forward. The perspective and mindset that you have on your life is what can drive your success and see the growth of what you want to see in your life.

The next question that needs to be addressed is the idea if there is a type of person that needs seeing a counselor the most... The LMHC's response was "Somebody who is at a safety risk of self-harm or harming others and or is being released from a psychiatric hospitalization" (LMHC). This is important to think about because there are a lot of people who face these feelings and can be prevented if there are steps that are taken. Following up regularly with a mental health counselor that helps guide your journey and gives you advice on your life can help give your life more clarity. The idea of getting out of the psychiatric hospital: I have been there. I know what it is like to be lonely and stuck while getting out of the hospital and trying to comeback 2 success.

Giving it your all is what really matters. The results will be found by the effort that you put into yourself and your life. If you are constantly worrying and wondering when and how your life can change, it is up to you to choose how you respond to these feelings. The feelings are only temporary. As a result, it is important to give yourself grace and provide yourself with the support needed to avoid feeling in an unstable mindset. When I asked the LMHC "Do you have any other feedback that you wanted to share that relates to mental health and counseling?" His response was "Great benefit for potentially anyone and everyone" (LMHC). The benefit can be found for anyone because we all want to be heard and want to see our lives succeed. We all have ways on how our life can be improved upon. Talking to someone and helping them get their thoughts out there can be of great benefit in your life.

The next and final question that I posed to the LMHC was "What are some ways our community can open more access?" Their response was "Managed care and health insurance companies could credential and panel (Group of providers) more licensed providers" (LMHC). This is a great point because from my own experience, I found that it was a struggle at times finding the right provider that I could use based on the insurance that I had. For many, I believe that this is the same case. A similar scenario is the lack of coverage limits the patient to a wider variety of options for counselors who can be of great value to their lives (Amber Geer talks about this as well).

Managed care is something where you can develop stability in your life and create structure that enables you as an individual rather than disabling. This is something to think about when deciding how you want to live your life. Using the resources like insurance to help give you the tools needed to learn to live freely is priceless.

The panel or group of providers is something that is incredibly important for giving others an opportunity to get access to the care needed to succeed.

After interviewing Dr. Jantz it was interesting hearing his perspective on how the mental health industry is being impacted. His book Healing Depression For Life has a lot of fundamentals that helps you gain insight on how to battle against depression. He references this a lot of times. The interesting part about his answers were that they were all clear and concise. Dr. Jantz is founder of A Place of Hope in Edmonds, Washington where the center helps patients with depression, mental health struggles, addiction and many more.

Brandon: "Dr. Jantz, what has been your biggest accomplishment throughout your career in mental health"?

Dr.Jantz: "Growth of the Center A Place of Hope. International influence in the area of whole person care" (Dr.Jantz). This Place of Hope has been a foundation for help and care to help rehabilitate others who have struggles with mental health and depression.

Dr.Jantz's educational background includes "...doctorate in counseling and psychology"

Brandon: "What are the biggest struggles that the world is facing right now related to mental health?"

Dr.Jantz: "Due to the pandemic, depression and anxiety. WHO (World Health Organization) says that depression is a worldwide problem" (Dr. Jantz). This is something that the World Health Organization has even declared as something that needs to be changed. There are a lot of people out there right now that are struggling with depression and are trying to find a way in their life. Finding their passion and happiness can be a hard and long process. The struggles of life that come along with depression and anxiety are so hard to accept. The only thing we can all do when this comes our way is to reach out for help and gain support from family, friends or mental health professionals.

The next question talks about how future mental health professionals can make a positive imprint on the clients and mental health industry. I ask, Brandon: "For those in higher education, what is the best piece of advice you could give students to help achieve results that will be long lasting for achieving mental health goals?"

Dr.Jantz: "A lot of opportunities in the field of mental health. Be encouraged about the future opportunity. You are needed."

Brandon: You have a great opportunity to help a lot of people get the help they need to stay on top of their goals. When you recognize that your life can make a very big impact on someone who is coming in or out of a crisis. The opportunities that I know based on my experience of being a client includes a Case Manager, Psychiatrist, nurse, receptionist and many more.

The next question that I ask is "For those that are trying to comeback 2 success, what advice can you give to someone who was faced with a mental illness or health condition?" Dr.Jantz's response was "Recovery is always possible and with all of our pain comes great opportunity. Opportunity to change other peoples life." As a result, everyone has the power and ability to comeback 2 success from their struggles in life. Whether it be mental health struggles or anything that is creating conflict in their life.

There are a lot of things that the nation is trying to do to help make a positive and more openly accepted place. Dr.Jantz goes into some ideas of his perspective of the progress with accepting addictions that someone is experiencing.

Dr.Jantz: "Addiction field, first there was a lot of shame. Now it is okay to talk about shame. They are talking about getting help. Encouraging to get the word out that it is okay to ask for help." The addiction field is so prevalent and makes a deep imprint on the lives of many with mental health struggles. From my experiences of living with bipolar, addictions are a key thing that needs to be addressed and changed to create a more stable individual that can function at an optimal level like they were created to do.

The final question that I asked Dr.Jantz was " For those that are pursuing med school or any type of higher education, what can students do to make a positive change as they gain more knowledge, experience and expertise in the mental health industry?" His response was "Themes through the book "Healing Depression For Life". Great opportunity to spread the words of hope. Plan for people's wellness by asking for help and getting good care we can help encourage." This is something that we can all do to help create a more sustainable and wholesome society. The ideas inside the book are a foundation to the fundamentals for overcoming depression. For those that are studying, the book premise focuses on "The Personalized Approach that Offers New Hope for Lasting Relief".

Who is the best support system that can help improve the lives of the adolescent with a mental health diagnosis or imbalance?

Peer to Peer interview with Matt McGaha: Perspective on Mental Health Diagnosis as an adolescent.

Questions to ask Matt:

Date: February 18, 2020

Time: 6:30pm

Brandon: What is your mental health diagnosis?

Matt: Bipolar 1 disorder

Brandon: When did this occur?

Matt: First experienced symptoms in 6th grade. 11 or 12 years old. First diagnosed at 14 years old.

Brandon: How has it impacted your life?

Matt: Manifested itself as a struggle in the early years. Has been something that I can't ignore but I have always strived to live with it and be successful.

Brandon: What is the main objective that you are doing to maintain a happy and healthy lifestyle?

Matt: Taking my meds as prescribed. Attending medical appointments. Living a clean life.

Brandon: What advice would you give to someone who has recently been struggling with mental health and is trying to comeback 2 success?

Matt: Reach out for help if you haven't already. You can do this. There is hope.

Brandon: Any other thoughts you might have that you would like to share with the reader?

Matt: Many people who are successful and or famous as well as your everyday person have lived with and overcome this life struggle as well. You can do this. Take it a step at a time. You are loved by at least some family and friends. Try to acknowledge the love and support that you have in your life.

Brandon: How do you learn to overcome the stigma that exists in mental health?

Matt:I try to not take everything so personally, especially when it comes to judgement and mistreatment. And neglect. Opening up to others who may have been going through the same things as you. Not forgetting that you have a voice.

After interviewing Matt McGaha, he shared his opinion about how he was overcoming his obstacles and aimed to comeback 2 success. As for the best form of recovery, he expressed his opinion on how to be successful in spite of a mental health struggle and past addiction problem. Matt says "Everybody has their own path, own journey...Has their own version of what their recovery will look like... varies from person to person" (McGaha). When you choose to recognize that everyone has their own path and choices that will get them back to where they want to, life gets better for you. From the client perspective for mental health, it is up to the individual to use their voice and state the needs of what they feel is necessary to cultivate a healthy and smart recovery.

In the interview with Matt, we covered another question: "What is the best way for mental health professionals to provide their clients with impactful support?" Matt's response was "Continuing to be there and be relatable about how their clients are... be someone that they can confide in and also doesn't act better than... sharing their life experiences because it shows the client can empathize and cares... gain the clients trust" When I was just starting out seeing a case manager, I found that I was not sure where to start at being open and sharing my feelings with someone who I barely knew.As a community, we need to learn how to erase the stigma that exists for others who have a struggle and are trying to create relationships with the community that fosters excellence and commitment to a brighter future. Relying on someone to overcome your obstacles will help you gain more perspective on yourself and understand what you need to do to prevent another relapse.

It all starts with you as an individual. Use your voice and actions to reach for help and overcome the stigma that it takes to get out of your bad habits and get out of your comfort zone that will help you succeed. When I was living in the halfway house and things were so miserable, it seemed like there were times when I didn't feel like the struggle was ending. The best piece of advice that I stuck with was the fact that I kept going and took life one step at a time. Patience is a virtue. For example, because I was stuck living in the halfway house, I chose to go to the mental health program in Atlanta, Georgia where I could be successful and promote a positive growth that would have a life long lasting impact on my mental health and life for the future.

The next interview I get a chance to speak with a volunteer at NAMI Whatcom County:

Amy Armstrong

MA Biomedical Sciences

BA Psychology

Date: May 12, 2020

Time: 12:30pm

Brandon: What inspired you to want to help others with mental illnesses and struggles?

Amy: Most inspired by having own background with mental health struggles. Helping give others the opportunity to recover and live well with their mental health issues. Help people to help themselves.

Brandon: What are some of the pieces of advice you could give to others who want to comeback 2 success when faced with a mental health struggle?

Amy: Important to try to give themselves compassion, time and patience to know that it is not a straight path. There are a lot of ups and downs. It is normal and okay. You can be strong in working with these things and that you are not alone. Seek support

Brandon: How can you use your voice to help make a positive change in society with how stigma is dealt with?

Amy: Sharing your own story, sharing about statistics, expressing that you are open for people to talk with. Talking about it. Starting the conversation.

Brandon: What has been your favorite part about helping inspire others with mental health struggles or illness struggles?

Amy: Seeing the changes that have happened, seeing the strengths. Seeing the people come to a place where they realize that there shouldn't be stigma around mental health.

Brandon: If you could give someone with a mental illness or advice, what fundamentals could you offer them?

Amy: Realizing that you matter is one thing. Realizing that your life matters. Reaching out to someone whether it is a friend, a teacher, a family member, a therapist and say "hey, I am struggling" "is it okay that we talk about this?" Finding things that help you and knowing that it differs from person to person. For what someone might find helpful might not be helpful for you. Treating yourself with the compassion that you would treat a loved one. Realizing that you deserve love. The things that you say to yourself to who you love. You wouldn't judge the person for what they are struggling with. Be treated well. Advocate for yourself. Never give up hope.

Brandon: After interviewing Amy, there were a lot of general themes that were painted as a picture. The first is that mental health is a place where more attention is needed for support from others. Also, NAMI is a place where anyone can find help with mental health struggles. NAMI is a welcoming and judgment free environment that is welcoming to help you in your recovery or support to overcome your mental health struggles.

There is something that is profound when a group of people come together to bring their struggles to the table and help build each other up by moral support. Amy's role in the support group is to help be a facilitator and help guide the various topics for the group.

When interviewing Amy, we discussed the idea of finding inspiration and motivation to help others in the mental health industry, she referenced the idea of helping others to help themselves. There are some things that we can do to help us focus on our recovery and success in life. Longevity is key. Following up with mental health professionals is the way to get things moving in the right direction. There are certain things that might be out of your control.

Those that have had mental health struggles and are trying to comeback 2 success is a big question that I addressed to Amy. Her response was "follow the straight path" which I articulated by focusing on what you can do in your life and reach out for help if you think you need it. You are your best advocate for your life. Your voice is powerful and you have the ability to find success in overcoming the road of recovery.

There are mental health organizations all around the country. All you need to do is google "mental health organization near me" and see what pops up. The next thing that is important is how you can gain so much from the changes and work that people have put into themselves to be better. Finding your strength and playing on it from within is the best piece of advice that I can give based on my recovery and life journey.

Lastly, when it comes to the interview with Amy, "you deserve to be loved" and have the help to gain insight so that you can be better than you were yesterday. There is no better place to start than to have a conversation with someone that is close to you. You have the chance to get up and find peace within yourself and find joy again if you are willing to put in the hard work for your recovery. When you reach your recovery point, then it is a matter of maintaining that so that you can be successful and find strength to chase your wildest dreams and goals in your life.

Amber Geer Interview:

- Brandon: Tell us a little bit about yourself...

Amber: 28 years old. Go to Northwest University Online Program. Soccer is my passion. Bachelor's degree from Seattle Pacific University 2018 Bachelors of Arts in Psychology

- Brandon: What have you learned about the mental health industry since enrolling in your classes to become a counselor?

Amber:Since enrolling into the graduate program at Northwest University

- Amber: Everyone shows symptology, can lead to underdiagnosis and misdiagnosis.

- Amber: Abnormal Psychology, eye opening class

  ○ Biological, DNA/genetic predisposition to mental health/illness

  ○ Nurtured: the environment you grew up in, live in, how that impacts your ability process emotions, engage, be in relation with people, etc. "ATTACHMENT THEORY"

- Amber: What are the most important topics or ways of thinking that need to be discussed for students pursuing a career in mental health?

    a. Ways of thinking: open minded, critical thinking skills,

    b. Genuineness, self reflection; being aware of potential <u>transference and counter transference</u>

- Brandon: How can the mental health industry be changed in a positive way to better develop care and recovery for those affected by mental illness?

Amber: Access and advocacy are the biggest challenges that this nation is facing.

- Brandon: How can the schools better teach students about mental health?

Amber: Teachers need to be aware and educated about mental health. Open to the concept and have a basic understanding of what to do when a child says to you "I am feeling sad..."

- Brandon: Why is there such a high level of people who are struggling with mental health problems?

Amber: We are entering a world where it is okay to start talking about mental health and seeing that there are so many of us that struggle. Developing as a society where it is more okay with having a mental illness.

- Brandon: What needs to change in the nation to help people overcome their addictions, depression and other mental illnesses?

Amber: Better access and insurance needs to be less restrictive for giving out diagnosis and longer time to see the therapist or mental health professionals.

- Brandon: You mentioned that you are going to school for counseling... How can counseling add value to someone who is struggling with their mental health?

Amber: Added support to the client's support system. There are some clients who come in with no support system. Counseling is part of the management of your symptoms. Counseling is not for everybody.

What works best for you and your life. **Finding what works best for you and your mental illness.**

It was a great opportunity to interview Amber Geer. This interview gave me more insight into how, from a grad student perspective, the mental health industry is changing and how education institutions need to change dramatically in order to help students understand the importance of mental health. Amber is 28-years old, goes to Northwest University and graduated from Seattle Pacific University in 2018 with a Bachelors of Arts in Psychology.

"Access and advocacy are the biggest challenges that this nation is facing." This is something that has such an incredible impact on how things need to be changed in the mental health community. Society and the government needs to realize that there are necessary changes to be made and that funding is needed in order to make some monumental strides that can help millions.

Amber emphasized the importance of providing teachers with training so as to make them more conscious of education as related to mental health. She states, "Teachers need to be aware and educated about mental health. Open to the concept and have a basic

understanding of what to do when a child says to you"
"I am feeling sad…"

I posed a very relevant question on what the nation needs to implement to see results.. Amber said, "What needs to change in the nation to help people overcome their addictions, depression and other mental illnesses? Better access and insurance needs to be less restrictive for giving out diagnosis and longer time to see the therapist or mental health professionals". Therapists are critical for helping those with mental health struggles gain new perspectives. They focus on engaging their clients in important conversation that there can be positive results in the community thriving.

Finally, the last question that I asked Amber was, "You mentioned that you are going to school for counseling… How can counseling add value to someone who is struggling with their mental health?" Amber's response was, "Added support to the client's support system. There are some clients who come in with no support system. Counseling is part of the management of your symptoms. Counseling is not for everybody. What works best for you and your life." Finding what works best for you and your mental health.

I think that Amber hit the nail on the head when she said, "Finding what works best for you and your mental illness". For those suffering with a mental illness, this is a decision that only you can make. Following a strict regimen that can help you focus on yourself and gain perspective on yourself can have positive impacts

Interviewee: Zack

Date:

Time:

B: Zack, could you tell us a little bit about yourself? What is your educational background?

Z: I received my bachelor's degree in psychology and my master's degree in clinical mental health counseling. I completed my 3 years of required post-graduation supervision in 2018 and subsequently became fully licensed in Georgia as a LPC (licensed professional counselor).

B: What impact does mental health programs like Skyland trail have on someone dealing with a mental illness?

Z: I feel like there are many considerations to take into account when considering how impactful, either positive or negative, a mental health program, like

Skyland Trail can have. A few factors to consider would be: is the program an appropriate clinical fit for the mental illness in which you are struggling, is it a credible program that follows evidenced based practices, is the client ready and willing to fully participate in the program? If these factors are appropriately considered, then I believe a mental health program like Skyland Trail can have a tremendous positive impact in one's life. It has the potential to provide with the appropriate level of intensive care to help them better manage their mental illness.

B: What is the goal of Skyland trail when helping their client's comeback 2 success?

Z: I think this is best expressed by our mission, "Offering hope, changing lives." I feel our goal for every client seeking our services is to leave with a better understanding of themselves and their future goals and understanding that while their mental health diagnosis may play a role in that, it does not define who they are. We want every client to leave with the appropriate skills to manage their mental health and to feel confident in their ability to live a happy and successful life.

B: What is the best approach that a mental health organization can do to help their clients battling with a mental illness or mental health struggle?

Z: I believe that it starts and ends with compassion. Taking the time to understand them as a whole person, and not just their mental illness, is key. Then using that information to treat the whole person psychologically, medically, nutritionally and psychically. This is something I believe Skyland Trail does exceptionally well.

B: How can society learn to grow and move forward to be more accepting for individuals with a mental illness?

Z: I believe that it all starts with building awareness through education and training. People are always going to fear the things they do not fully understand, so with more funding to provide education and trainings, we would be able to start moving in the right direction.

B: What value does Skyland trail enrich in someone's life if they attended a place like a mental health program?

Z: I believe that Skyland Trail believes in ultimately helping clients identify their values and then helping them better cultivate them in their daily lives. In my experience, one value that run through all of the work we do is self-love. We want to help people not only accept themselves, but to love themselves and recognize how their gifts positively impact their world and those around them.

B: How have you and Skyland trail grown since its first opening back in 1989?

Z: Skyland Trail has been in operation for over 30 years. Over the years it has grown to span multiple campuses, recently expanding to include adolescents aged 14-17, and offer evidenced based treatment to both adults and adolescents with complex psychiatric diagnoses. Personally, I attribute so much of what I have learned about mental health and effective forms of treatment to my time at Skyland Trail. Working at Skyland Trail has helped me grow not only as a clinician, but as a more well-rounded person. I am more confident in my abilities and cannot speak highly enough of the training and support I have received from them since I began working at Skyland in 2015.

B: As we look forward into the future, how can we as a community learn to grow and create more acceptance of others with a mental health diagnosis?

Z: This a great question, with many possible answers depending on whom you ask. I maintain that building awareness through education and trainings is going to be the best increase people's knowledge of mental health. With education, comes understanding and with understanding, the hope would be that acceptance would follow. I think there have been efforts made, and there is much more that needs to be done. It will not be an easy task and it will mean getting support from community and government leaders at varying levels of influence.

6. Atomic Habits for Mental Health

Without the desire to get better and to have a happier life, your diagnosis will hinder you. Any alcohol and drugs consumed only heighten and ramp up the symptoms of your mental health condition. All the while, you are feeling low, depressed and might be faced with a lack of control. Life only gives us so many friends that will keep us close and encourage us to be happy and successful.

Take advantage of the fact that someone loves you, cares about you and wants to see you change. Only you get to choose how you want to try and do that. Every person diagnosed with a mental illness has a choice on how they handle it. Your diagnosis doesn't define you. You have the daily opportunity to focus on what you can do to overcome the diagnosis and carry yourself on the way to success.

Taking responsibility for your life starts with understanding your diagnosis. If you don't sacrifice some of your time and energy to learn about how you can control your mental health struggle, there will be long-lasting negative results. Getting out of old habits can be hard. The support from others can help alleviate this struggle.

The book *Atomic Habits Summary* by James Clear was very informative and discussed the ways in which developing good habits lead to success.

An example of this is how many people with a mental illness choose to use alcohol and narcotics to cope with their symptoms. This habit is hard to break. In the book *Summary of Atomic Habits: An Easy and Proven Way to Build Good Habits and Break Bad Ones*, James Clear states "Habits that are long established but destructive are very hard to change for several reasons...people tend to try to change the wrong thing and also approach it in the wrong way" (Clear 19). We choose to live but implement bad behaviors that lead us to feeling empty.

When I was lonely and lost while in the hospital, I got to ponder why I didn't reach out for help or guidance from others. When people choose to isolate themselves from others and rely solely upon themselves, they have a higher risk of not having a successful and happy life.

Mental illness can be controlled using some of James Clear's fundamentals. Another point that Clear brings up is how individuals have been faced with a predisposition. He states, "Predispositions certainly do not determine outcomes, but they can be manipulated for advantage" (Clear 89). In other words, the biggest realization you can make when you are diagnosed with a mental illness is the fact that you as an individual have the power to accept where you are at and not let the negativity and symptoms prevent you from going out and pursuing what you want. Following this, it is all about developing a habit that will lead to more good habits. Creating a routine will also be helpful in your journey .

Clear makes a lot of great points about how to foster good habits that result in success and overall happiness. As you continue on this journey, it is important that you give yourself grace and can be open to failure when things aren't going your way. Another example of how you can start developing happy and healthy habits is through your willingness to make bad habits impossible: "sometimes you can get better results by making bad habits impossible than by trying to make good habits easier" (Clear 68). This can look like reducing your ability to focus on your bad habit. Your ability to engage in healthy habits determines your level of success. This is because you need to have the stability to focus on the things that matter the most to you. Your ability to control your behaviors and seek positivity is the key to unlocking your truest potential and happiness .

I have attended multiple group therapy sessions where I got to hear other people's stories and how they have been dependent on things that have led them down the wrong path. The hard part about it is that many people choose to stay "stuck" in a way of thinking that limits their ability to succeed. Sure alcohol and narcotics are very prevalent; they are an easy way to cope with negative feelings that exist. However, it is up to the individual to focus on engaging in good habits that have a transformative effect. Based on my conversations with other people who have a mental illness, the hardest part that people avoid is their ability to embrace their failures and struggles. People are filled with shame and sadness about their past so they don't move on and find a way to have a better and happier tomorrow. With that being said, don't let the negativity and stigma of reaching out for help prevent you from being at peace within your heart, mind, body and soul.

Enjoy the things that make you feel alive and give you a reason to wake up every morning. This can change over time. The ability to establish good habits can make you unstoppable and resilient regardless of your mental health condition. I have demonstrated my resilience and commitment to a dream that has come to life.

Everyone makes Impulsive decisions. However, those that have been diagnosed with a mental illness are more susceptible to making choices that aren't necessarily helpful.

Impulsive decisions create more problems than need to be. You can focus on getting support from family, friends and mental health professionals to make sure that your mind is on the right track for success. We can't control what life throws at us. However, we can control how we react to circumstances.

Impulsive decisions can create a lot of damage in our lives. They can hurt others that are close to us and, in turn, create a lot of distance that discourages growth. Very rarely is it a good idea to take things really fast. As they say, the turtle wins the race. Planning for your future and focusing on one step at a time is the best thing to do.

Mental health and addictions:

Many people choose to self-medicate in ways that aren't conducive to a healthy and happy lifestyle.

This can consist of using drugs, alcohol and engaging in other addictions. Confronting that you have a problem is the first step. I have been inside of many group therapy sessions where people say they are going to stop smoking or drinking. Instead, they choose to self-medicate and create a vicious cycle of habits. The habits are dragging them down. My worst habit was choosing to not accept that I had Bipolar Disorder. It took over 4 years until I finally came to a level of acceptance. Since then, I don't feel as dragged down and controlled by something.

There might be addictions that are getting in the way of you pursuing your passion. When this is the case, the best advice I can give you is to reach out to someone. There are groups out there like Narcotics Anonymous (NA) and Alcoholics Anonymous (AA). I am here to say that you can get up and put your passion in front of your addictions. Once this starts to happen, life starts to change and you can find real success.

As I talked about earlier, the failures that you endure will only make you stronger if you are willing to accept the struggles that go along with failing. I have learned that the failures and mistakes that I have made in my life have helped me to become a better person and more aware as to what I need to do to stay humble, consistent and to effectively live my life.

There will be people that tell you to take the safe route and to not strive for the biggest and best dreams. I have had family members tell me what I can and can't do. The bottom line is that you are the one that defines your future. You can achieve your work and life goals. The failures will come and go if you are willing to give yourself grace and empathy .

Life lessons are learned every day. You can choose to stay in your old ways that get you close to nowhere or you can choose to make a change.This change could inspire the passion and strength you need to persevere and find the results that you are looking for.

Failures can get in your way if you let them. The first time that I got outside of the hospital, I moved into my old roommates house in Everson, Washington. I was weak as hell from the lack of exercise and non-nutritious disgusting hospital food. I decided that I was not defeated when I was let out of the hospital. I decided that I was going to keep trying and see what the world had to offer. I wanted to be more successful than I was willing to accept the pain, sadness and discomfort that I was going through. As I laced up my shoes, tears rolling down my face, I told myself "you can do this". One step at a time. Eventually, I was outside in the summer heat. Running with the wind in my face as trucks and cars went whizzing past on Noon Road.

It was then that I realized that life is like a game. We are the main players, and we have resources that we can use to get us to where we want to go. The result should be happiness and success. You are in control of your life and your actions. Living with my roommate was an incredible learning opportunity. I found myself growing a lot but lonely at the same time. There were times when I didn't know what and where to go with my life. I worked at McDonald's for a month or so which helped me to support myself. Somedays, before work, I found myself crying as I listened to motivational speakers. I was struggling to find motivation given all the pain and discomfort that I had been in.

Whatever circumstances came out of the failures, it has made me who I am, and I can say that I am stronger and much wiser when making decisions. If you don't make errors in life, how will you learn? When I was in the hospital, I had time to think about the challenges that I went through and try my best to stay sane. Fighting against yourself is not the way to live a happy and healthy lifestyle. The mindset that I have every day is to give myself grace for failing and learning from my mistakes. There is so much to be grateful for, depending on the perspective that you have. I have struggled so much but this allows me to say that you are not defined by your past. You can move onward to brighter days and find success in your own way.

7. Fundamental plan for living a happy and healthy lifestyle with a mental illness diagnosis

You may be asking yourself, is it possible to prevent yourself from getting a mental illness? Unfortunately, most of the time being diagnosed with a mental illness is out of your control and often comes from your family heritage. Life is all about balance. I recommend that you try getting into a routine that will help you live a healthy lifestyle. The bottom line is that no one is susceptible to a diagnosis but you can choose to manage your symptoms by creating sustainable habits. As mentioned earlier, there is much to gain in your life when you maintain a healthy diet and sleep. Finally, having someone as an accountability partner to help you reach your mental health goals will help you increase the chances of fulfilling them.

Painful rejection by society often comes when diagnosed with a mental illness. I personally understand that a mental health diagnosis can add an additional challenge to your life. It often feels like a wave of difficulties are drowning you. I am here to tell you that everything is going to be okay. You may not have power to control whether or not you have a mental illness but you do have the power to control yourself and your choices.

Down Time:

When dealing with a mental health diagnosis like bipolar, I find myself needing to set aside time to relax and recharge my brain. This looks different for different people. The act of caring for yourself by giving yourself downtime to relax and rest is important for anyone who is dealing with a mental illness. It is hard to give yourself time to just relax when life gets in the way.

By giving yourself downtime you will benefit by becoming a healthier and happier you. You can learn how your body works and recognize what your prime hours to function are in a day. Downtime can be used to reflect on your life and the day. After moving to Seattle, WA and Cerritos, California, after work I choose to make time to recharge my battery by dedicating time to read, write or talk with close friends. The act of going out of your way to dedicate time for yourself to reflect and recharge is the definition of self-love/care.

Every day you have the choice to live a balanced life while seeking your goals and dreams. Downtime is crucial for anyone who is trying to Comeback 2 Success and overcome their daily struggles that happen in life. When I got out of the hospital, I had to give myself a lot of time to recharge my battery by sleeping.

Some examples of downtime activities that have helped me include working out, cooking, cleaning, talking on the phone, reading, writing and sleeping. There are a plethora of other ideas that exist out there. The point is, it is up to you to try and discover what works for you and keeps you in balance. The act of giving yourself downtime makes you a better person who is more well-rounded and able to function in the ups and downs of life. You control your energy level and how you respond to the external circumstances that life throws at you. Everyone needs time to recharge their brain, to express how you feel and to recognize that you need to sacrifice time everyday to keep your body and mental health in sync. Life is a marathon not a sprint. I understand that grinding is something that we all want to do. However, it is the act of how you balance your busy lifestyle with the capacity of what your mental health can handle. Moral of the story: to not let the opinions of others get in the way of what you determine to be your own balance and lifestyle. It is up to you and the mental health professionals that you work with to help guide your life and establish a routine to help keep your body and mind healthy.

Downtime is a crucial thing that we all need as human beings. Learning how to give your body and mind the attention it needs will help prepare you for the daily grind. I highly recommend trying different hobbies and activities that will help you discover what works for you as you learn how to discover what works for your mental health. In the article "Why It's Important to Schedule More Downtime for Your Brain" Beth Janes states the fundamentals of downtime. She states," Take action, ignore your phone, be a little less connected, choose nature over concrete, peace out and follow your bliss" (Janes). I bring up this quote because Jane paints the picture clearly for what we need as humans to recharge our brains and get us to the next level in life. The most important thing that I believe you can do to have a happy and healthy life is to take action. I encourage you to take the first step today and follow the steps of what Beth Janes recommends.

Developing a Care Plan:

Having a care plan to manage your mental health helps to bring structure to your life when things aren't going well with your mental health. For example, when

I was at Skyland Trail in Atlanta, Georgia, they provided me with the opportunity to develop my own care plan catered towards my needs and aspirations in life. The care plan should help guide you towards being a better you instead of burdening you.

Care plans have many important features like establishing who will be your persons of contact when you are feeling low or mentally unstable. It is up to you to decide who your persons of support will be. Another important aspect is having a record of what hospital you want to go to in the event that you need professional help. When developing a care plan, think critically about what will be helpful to you and will empower you to face the mental health struggles you have been diagnosed with. It is critical that you reflect upon yourself by establishing realistic and attainable goals that will guide you in the right direction towards a happy and healthy recovery.

Another important topic about having a care plan includes the importance of relying on other people for help. Your care plan is there for you to fall back on on the hard days. Your family and friends that have been integrated into your care plan are crucial to helping you succeed. Humbling yourself to reach out to others when in times of need will help you achieve balance and overcome your instability.

Care plans are helpful when you develop them with someone. You are the most important author of your care plan because only you know what you need and want in your life. As a result, reaching out to others who know you very well can be a major asset in your life and help you in many ways as you focus on establishing a successful care plan. Don't feel bad if you don't have all the answers. Consider it a good opportunity to reach out to someone else that might have a good perspective and who can help guide you through this part of your journey in life.

Care plans are meant to encourage growth and success as you are moving onto the next stage of your life. You have a choice for how you want to respond to your times of crisis. I like to think of a care plan as a navigator in your life that can add value and stability that is crucial during times of uncertainty. If you don't know where to get started, care plans can be found easily online. There are a variety of templates that exist to help you can focus on improving yourself and follow steps towards a healthy recovery.

In my recovery, my care plan was something I used to help guide me in times of need. When I didn't have a person to reach out to, I could read the pamphlet and scan what ideas I had written down on paper to make a good judgment call for what I should be doing next to help myself.

Finally, a care plan is a valuable tool that can help you focus on yourself and accomplish your goals. When you are in a rough spot, writing your thoughts down on paper and following the template of a care plan can have a tremendous impact on your journey. Other important parts of the care plan include what your typical day looks like and what you look like when you are feeling like your healthiest self. Another important part is that you have signs of when you are feeling a way that isn't healthy.

Another routine that should be exercised is joining a club or group activity to help you get more engaged with the community. There are certain apps that exist out there like Meetup that provides you with many options for groups that you can join. In my recovery, I found it very helpful being around people. Going to my church and hearing the pastor talk was one way I got involved in my community and felt a deeper connection with my faith.

Your routine is the structure you create in your life that will help you overcome the struggles that come with having a mental illness. I want to encourage you to start taking steps towards self-care and establishing structure in your life that will help get you to where you want to go. The key is that you have to be the one willing to take the first step. This is always the hardest part. There will be days when you want to stay in bed or just feel like giving up. Heck, for me, there were so many times that I gave myself empathy as I slept in a lot to recharge my battery to give me energy to start working.

The bottom line is that we as human beings can accomplish much more than we think. When faced with a relapse from mental health symptoms and trying to succeed, it is vital to focus on your inner self and what you can do one step at a time to live a happier and fulfilled life.

Fundamentals For Living a Happy and Healthy Lifestyle While Being Diagnosed With a Mental Illness:

The following list is laid out in order of importance. First, you need sleep to help you function and thrive in life. This looks like getting an average of at least 8 hours of sleep. When recognizing this, it is important to also set a sleep schedule that you can stay on top of to help your body get into a regular routine. Sleep is what helps your cognitive abilities function at an optimal level. Without it, we are prone to errors and mistakes that don't lead to a happy and healthy lifestyle.

When it comes to working on yourself, establishing a regular sleep habit will get you further than you think.

When you have a mental health condition like bipolar disorder, sleeplessness can occur. When you are experiencing any type of mania or depressive state, sleep can be difficult. This is why it is critical to reach out for help when you acknowledge this is what your body is experiencing. What to do when you are lacking sleep? Reach out for help from a family or friend. If the sleep doesn't stop, reach out for help from a mental health professional. Take the first step and sacrifice your discomfort for trying to succeed in your own way. Acknowledging and accepting that there are other options and ideas out there that exist that help others focus on their sleep will help you stay optimistic about how you can overcome the irregular sleep patterns.

When everything seems to be out of control and you are struggling to take hold and control of your life, it is critical to take a step back and narrow down on the things that you can control. When you do this, isolating the things that you can't control will help you engage more with the things that you can control.

Another fundamental that is important to think about is the fact that you have a choice for how you want to experience your care. Your responsibility is to gain perspective and guidance from others who have wisdom and experience in working with your feelings and worries. Your choices dictate who you want to be and how your life will turn out.

Next, your diet is something that you should consider and keep in mind to have a healthy brain. Some examples of eating healthy may look like eating a lot of fruits and vegetables. Meat is an important part of my diet like chicken, ham and turkey. Avoiding sugary things can be hard, but it is worth it and can make a significant impact on your mental health. I splurge every now and then but within moderation.

Exercise is something that I want to introduce as a fundamental way to control your mental illness. This is something that we all need as humans. Exercise helps us release endorphins and let go of stress. I have found it very helpful in stressful times at work to do things actively like running or playing soccer. This elevated my mood significantly. When you are in a good mood, the world is your oyster. There is nothing getting in your way besides yourself. Some examples of exercise for you could be swimming, running, soccer, walking, basketball, football, biking and weight lifting. Many forms of activities exist out there that will help you relieve pressure and tension that your body has built up over time. When your body is happy, this can combat the negative feelings that your brain is experiencing. Mental illnesses can be combated with a double dose of exercise that will help remedy any type of symptoms.

In sum, proper rest has proven to help my brain and body function at an optimal level. Establishing a good sleep routine will help you stay on top of your goals and focus on reducing the likelihood of experiencing insomnia or restlessness. You are in the driver seat of your life. Take charge of that and recognize when you need something and want something. Go for it. There is nothing stopping you but yourself. Your responsibility as a person with a mental illness is to find your path in how you can overcome this with help from others. Mental health professionals or family and friends is a great place to start. The lows helped guide me into a path of success.

Once again, exercise is something that should be emphasized heavily. This is something that we all need to have as humans. Some choose to neglect this and as a result become overweight. When you are faced with mental illness, exercise helps relieve the stress and symptoms that come with your diagnosis. I am saying this from experience. When I was faced with a manic episode and manic depression, I ended up running a lot which helped my body get a hold of the large amount of disconnect that my brain and body was experiencing.

This disconnect is hard to understand because my brain was going through a large amount of discomfort and lost feelings. While my body didn't know how to handle and adjust. Running helps balance things out and focuses on wearing out your body so that your brain can rest and feel re-energized after proper recovery.

Mind, body and spirit is something that needs to be brought up as well. Your mind is what you have to control how you live your life. Your body is what you have to make the actions possible. If you have the mindset and put in the sweat to pursue your dreams and strive for a better life, you will see that it is just sitting around your corner. And finally, the spirit is your inner faith in something that is guiding you along your journey in life. For me, that is the spirit of Christ and God watching over me. God helps those who help themselves and you have to be the one who stands up for what you want and go and get it. Tune out the rest of the people who are in your life trying to discourage you from chasing your dreams.

Breaking down your mental health diagnosis can be a tough challenge because of the fact that the diagnosis is so foreign and unknown. We aren't born and told that we will have this diagnosis at this age. Life happens and the diagnosis comes along with the changes of seasons that occur. Our diagnosis isn't something that you should be afraid of or look down upon yourself. In fact, it is all in the mindset that you give yourself when interacting with the world in your life. Once you recognize how to maintain the diagnosis and remain in balance with yourself and your life, everything gets better and is more manageable.

In my experience of being diagnosed with Bipolar at the age of 19, I had a lot of denial. What I learned was that denial is not a healthy path to go down in my life when I have seen so much beauty and happiness in the world as a kid. This is part of life and living a lifestyle that is on path towards success. As a result, I am offering my recommendation to you on how you can learn to maintain your balance and accept where you are with your diagnosis.

Certain addictive things tend to help you cope with your diagnosis. However, this isn't a natural and healthy way of overcoming the symptoms of your mental health diagnosis. Alcohol and drugs is an outlet that a lot of people take. I am here to tell you that you don't need to rely on either as a coping mechanism. There are plenty of ways that you can blow some steam off your head and sit down and get some things off your chest in a healthy manner.

Another example could be doing something that makes you happy and finding fulfillment in life. Do it every day and your life will be inspired and motivated to make a difference. Running has helped me tremendously as I can blow off steam and get my emotions out on the road or trails. Life can be a struggle and if you don't learn to control your diagnosis and emotions, nothing will change.

When learning to understand your specific mental health diagnosis for the first time, it can be scary and also compel you to just want to be in the state of denial. That's what I did. As a result, I just continued down a path of destruction and where I had a lack of control over myself. Consult with another person about the way you feel about the diagnosis. As I reflect now, it is also beneficial if you reach out to someone who also has the same diagnosis as you can learn from them. It is your right to challenge the diagnosis and determine if you deep down think it is the right one. Every time it will be you to decide what it is you need to change within yourself and the things that you can't change. As a result, as I still am managing my bipolar, I reflect on the wisdom that my family gave me along with their encouragement to accept and understand my diagnosis.

Taking responsibility for your diagnosis and life means to take a hold of the challenges that you were faced with and turn the lemons into lemonade. Some outlets of support to help you understand where you are in your life comes from within your desire to win and succeed regardless of the struggle that you were faced with. Don't let a diagnosis like Bipolar or depression prevent you from chasing your dreams. Recognize that you have the innate ability to pursue your goals and reach for the stars.

You can't help others until you help yourself. If you want to be an influential person, you have to learn to be a leader and get your life handled and in control. Everyone has a story to tell. Your story is powerful if you recognize this from within. Think of your life like you were living it your last day. How would you want to live it? What would you want your legacy to be? Would you let a mental health diagnosis get in the way of your biggest goals and dreams? Many times, in my life, I have fallen to my knees. The ability to get knocked to the ground and stand back up will help you get stronger and reach for the potential that you have. Every day you have a choice for who you want to be and whether you choose to let your circumstances bring you down or help propel you into the person you want to be.

Your diagnosis is only a part of you. As I mentioned earlier, understanding your diagnosis is imperative in order for you to control it and not let it control you. Focus on what you can do to take control of your life and not let the symptoms and negativity prevent you from your potential. You have a chance every day to be a better person than you were yesterday. What are you doing now to up your game? Start small and then tackle the big goals and dreams as time continues to progress.

Music improves your mental health and is proven to be a coping strategy:

When I say that music saves, I mean it. All the sleepless nights that I had nobody who understood me and the heights I was trying to reach, music was there. All the days when I felt down because the world seemed to be crushing my spirit, music was there. All the people in my life that told me I couldn't go in my own lane, music was there to build me up. Music helps break barriers that you have built up in your mind. It helps unleash the truest potential that you have within yourself. I am here to encourage you to start listening to something that has substance for you and makes you feel alive.

The music is what has fueled me when times were rocky. There is a long list of opportunities of getting access to a whole bunch of music. Nowadays, we have sites like YouTube to give us full access to a wide range of music. As for apps, we now have Spotify, Apple Music and SoundCloud to help us live our lives to the fullest.

The genres that exist out there are limitless. Music helps us take ourselves on a journey where we are able to connect with something that helps us feel alive. The multitude of feelings that is part of life is where music has been able to connect with the human race. Music traces back to a long past in our history of mankind. I am here to tell you that if you start choosing a variety of options, you will find that they help you deeply connect with yourself more.

Music helped me stay positive in the midst of feelings of uncertainty, sadness and pain. The biggest piece of advice I can give you is to keep your ears open to hearing the voice of other people as they share their story through music. Your life changes when you can empathize and change the way you are understanding someone from a musical perspective. I remember listening to Logic and Florida Georgia Line when I was feeling depressed and needed some form of inspiration to keep going. That is the struggle of life. We never always have control with what is going on. However, we can control how our destiny is created by reacting to the experiences. Putting your pain into song and sharing it with others is courageous. Listening to the stories of other artists and the powerful messages and stories they have is what is so transformative for the community, nation and world.

Lyrics in songs can be powerful. They send a message and make statements about things such as life that helps us stay engaged in what the artist is saying. Music and the lyrics of many genres just make you feel good and help inspire you to be the best you can be in this world. Life is too short not to try and indulge yourself in a whole array of genres that this world has to offer. You get to choose who you are when you listen to the lyrics of the artists and compare yourself to them by hearing where they are at in their lives. The list goes on when you talk about some of the options of what people can do to learn from others through the lyrics of music. Music has a powerful effect on everyone regardless of your background. All over the world, we have different genres and types that help fuel each other's lives.

When going through a mental health crisis, music can be there to help you cope with your feelings and try to maintain a steady balance that is healthy.

When I was in the hospital, I found that Macklemore and Ryan Lewis were artists that helped keep me afloat. Human passion can be found at the root of the music that is accessible to humans. We as humans want to be understood. As a result, when dealing with a mental health struggle, music can be like your anchor in the stormy weather of life. I think it is wrong to deprive anyone of their right to listen to music and explore the aid that it can give freely to patients while being inside the hospital.

Self-care is something that is so valuable to the overall health of anyone. When you choose to commit time into things that are valuable and healthy for your recovery and overall well-being, you can see changes in your life that propel you to your success. Some examples of self care start with the physical health aspects.

Your physical health is something that should be addressed and well thought of to encourage overall well-being. The more stability you have, the more success you will have in your long term trajectory. Some examples of working on your physical health could look like joining a running club, taking swimming lessons, joining a sports team and training for a race.

Your diet is the next thing that needs attention. When you are eating right and fueling your body with energy to achieve your goals, your body will be happier and mental health will be improved. The diet is something that gives your body the fuel to have a balanced health. The diet really is a prime example of self care because you are giving needed attention to your body by providing yourself with the proper nutrition needed to reach your goals. By giving yourself food that isn't healthy and nutritious can put your body in a place where it is harder to crush your goals.

Your mental health is another very important aspect of self-care. You have the innate ability to engage in healthy mental health habits that will get you to where you want to go in life. Some examples of mental health habits include finding your coping mechanisms to keep you stable. Especially in times of a crisis, your mental health practices will set you up for success when things aren't always going your way. Other mental health habits that can be engaged in consist of reading books and how they have a lot of ideas on how to overcome your obstacles within yourself. Based on my experience, when I was in the hospital and mental health program, I found that reading was an escape from the struggles of life.

Reading helped me practice therapy without doing anything that would negatively impact my body.

Nobody said traveling would be easy. You can learn a lot more about yourself and how others react to your diagnosis by traveling and being openly receptive to the opinions of others. You are the product of your environment. Traveling is difficult for some who have a mental health problem. However, it is not impossible to fulfill a valued part of life that is enriching and rewarding in so many ways.

Spirituality and faith with mental health:

Finding your own faith or religion is something that can help you find peace in the midst of a lot of confusion and struggle with a mental illness. From my experience, I have found a lot of peace and understanding through accepting myself and my faith in Christ. The spirituality portion of life and for individuals struggling with a mental illness is what gives you peace of mind as you put your feelings and faith into something that is bigger than you. Spiritual and/or religious practices are out there. However, putting my faith in Christ has helped further my development in my life and has enriched my life spiritually.

While in the hospital, there are a lot of therapy sessions where spirituality was kind of opened up to explore upon and see the results that can happen through overall acceptance of oneself and peace of mind. There are books that are on spirituality that can help walk you through your journey in life and guide you in overcoming mental illness with coping strategies linked to your spirituality. My faith in Christ is what has helped me remain stable during the difficult times. I lean on the bible for strength.

In many ways, your spirituality is like the foundation and building blocks to your soul. For me, I was able to attend a lot of different classes on spirituality and freeing oneself from the negative energy to focus on healthy ways of thinking about myself that promoted peace, love and strength for one to be happy despite the mental illness that is present. Attending classes like this helps you further discover your clarity with a religion or another way of having perspective and acceptance. An example that I can really attest to was the classes that brought up peace, strength and tranquility as I was able to process my life through prayer. Also, a counselor or therapist can be someone who can help you explore this more.

The hospital focuses on more spiritual ways of coping with recovery than with religious ways.

Spirituality can come in many different ways. A big example looks like joining a type of religion or spiritual practice that seems to resonate well within yourself.

When I was struggling with heavy depression and anxiety, I was in a place where I was constantly testing my religion and was trying to decide what to believe in. This is a hard place to be in because there are so many unknowns and finding one's own sense of spirituality is a challenge for anyone to find peace and happiness in the midst of struggles with mental health. It almost felt like every day was a struggle to find peace within myself as I felt like I had nothing to believe in but the pound of my chest.

A big example of how I found my faith and strength in Christ was through the hard experiences when being in the psychiatric hospital. I already had a relationship with Christ. It was strengthened as I experienced a lot more pain and discomfort from fear of the unknown. I found myself struggling everyday to find peace within myself. Choosing a religion makes you feel at home and in a safe mental state. Historically speaking, religion can be very diverse yet controversial. The fact that there are so many religions and spiritual ways of thinking really doesn't limit anyone from trying and seeing what works best for them.

The steps to discovering your own spirituality and exploring yourself in a spiritual way can look like having a conversation with someone about how they feel about a certain religion or belief in something. Open conversations with others about your faith in something can help you by strengthening your faith as well.

Another good way of getting to know oneself and the spirituality that you might believe in is to attend some of the services and congregations. When I was studying abroad, my faith was tested because I was learning about so many different ways of thinking and struggled to find peace within myself as there were so many ideas and religions that seemed to have been mentioned by living in Europe.

The 12 steps program was a very insightful and helpful group that I was able to experience with other brothers in Christ. I was struggling getting out of the hospital in Winter of 2018. As a result, I decided to join the 12 steps program that was offered through my church group activities. This turned out to be a transformative experience as I have been able to relate well with others about how they tried to find peace and healing in Christ through their struggles.

Hearing other people and their struggles helps the feelings get better and focusing on how to create a positive atmosphere where you can find healing and growth through my own struggles with Bipolar Disorder. The 12 steps program is what helps individuals get help for their addictions or struggles in life and overcoming their obstacles through their faith in Christ supporting their journey. Just being involved with a group of men in Christ who are trying to find themselves again, see where they went wrong and how to become a better human being is powerful.

I found that the meetings were insightful as there were many opportunities to help share the faith and how you could overcome the mental health struggles that you were going through. I found that speaking out and sharing your voice is where you can see results happen as your life can change dramatically.

I was excited to show up because it was like my heart was out on the line sharing my experiences of mental health relapses over the two years. Finally, I made strides as I had some fellowship and support to help me overcome my obstacles as I looked forward into the future.

Faith in something can give you life in a way that earthly things and people can't give you. Reaching out to a mental health professional and pastor can be a good way to start overcoming your obstacles and struggles. This isn't very easy to digest as there can be so much pain and fear involved with overcoming the past struggles. Once you take life by the horns, you can reap the reward of peace inside your heart, body, mind and soul.

There were stages in the 12 steps program that gave you time to familiarize yourself with others and help gain perspective from other people as they shared what they felt like they needed to share. It is a 12 week program where you meet up with other members of the church to talk about the 12 steps and focus on what you can do to give yourself a successful recovery from a struggle or addiction. If you don't gain perspective and help to overcome your obstacles, it will be harder to get over the past errors and choices that have sometimes been out of your control.

The 12 steps program is where I found peace, happiness and tranquility as I was able to release my stress in a healthy way where I can gain perspective and ideas on how to navigate through my problems that gave me peace and light. My biggest encouragement for you if you are struggling with a mental health problem and are looking for something to believe in, sign up for a 12 steps program that is near you and see what it turns out to be. Or you can start one of your own in your church community. You can find a lot of peace and tranquility when you put yourself out there and find growth within your life that can help you gain peace and happiness. Listening to someone else's story is powerful and can be transformative for your life. Your faith in Christ can fill your cup up spiritually and you can find that the mental health portion will work together to help enrich and improve your life and daily goals.

Being a go getter with a mental illness can really help make a positive change in your life because you can create a life that is happy and fulfilling for you. Using your support system that can help guide you is always a plus to have. When you don't have a support system, it is good to take the responsibility for yourself and your needs by finding a reliable source of support to help you get the support you need for your life. Before you think about giving up, find within yourself the potential and grit you have that was blessed to you. You are stronger than you think.

The biggest reason to keep yourself going is to put your faith and life into something that is bigger than you and realize that you can accomplish your goals and dreams so long as you believe it. The mental health system is something that will drag you down if you let it. The bottom line is you should do whatever it takes to live a happy and healthy lifestyle.

When I am struggling to find motivation to fuel my passion, I always look up to god for giving me the right words to make the choices that will get me to where I want to go. Every day is a new opportunity. When you recognize that you have the ability to be successful in any field, life gets better.

You get to decide how open you want to be with your mental health condition. Sharing it with your co-workers is something that is important to think about. Ultimately, your choices will help make a positive change the more truthful you are with yourself and finding the confidence to speak up when you need to. We all have choices for how we want to be open about our diagnosis with others. For me, it was hard to do this because I had a lot of stigma and shame about being diagnosed with Bipolar Disorder. Instead I would compress the shame to the point where I would find struggles to be successful and my truest self at work.

Speaking up and sharing with the world what you want is the first step to stand up for what you want and reap the rewards of being authentic. Putting yourself out there and knowing that you might get rejected is something that is only learned through experience.

Trying is the hardest part to overcome your mental health struggles. Putting yourself in a place where you are ready to learn to earn your own freedom and to not let something prevent you from living out your dreams. A perfect example that I can share with you personally is why I moved to Seattle. Moving to Seattle sparked so much mental growth. I found out what I really want in life and what makes me happy and feel alive. Learning about myself in a major metropolitan city has helped me gain insight on what you can do to find your passion that fuels your growth and happiness.

Asking for help can come in many forms. Your verbal way of asking for help is a very effective way of doing it because you can help communicate your feelings to someone who should care about your feelings and wants to see you succeed. When you don't feel that you have a person to confide with, you need to keep searching for someone who will support you and give you the care that you need to overcome your mental health struggles. I have noticed that talking with someone can be one of the most liberating things to do yet also scary at the same time. Putting yourself out there and expecting rejection is not the mindset to have. You have to give yourself empathy for trying your best to focus on what you can control.

The next step to asking for help is to be patient. Patience is a virtue and for good reasons. Like I was saying earlier, things don't always change overnight. It is rare to see this. As a result, it is critical that you give yourself empathy, optimism and patience to wait for time to heal the scars of life and struggles that have been created within yourself. Bottom line is that you have a voice. Your voice matters and it is up to you for how you use it and want to see your life change or remain the same.

Asking for help can come in many forms. Asking for help is a very effective way to reach out because you can communicate your feelings to someone who cares about your feelings and wants to see you succeed. When you don't feel that you have a person to confide with, you need to keep searching for someone who will support you and give you the care that you need to overcome your mental health struggles. You have to give yourself empathy for trying your best to focus on what you can control.

Reaching out for help is something that we all struggle with. The biggest fear that we all have as humans is being rejected. Most of the time, we want to figure things out for ourselves in life. This is a great way to grow and personally develop. However, as humans, we need each other to overcome our struggles and rely upon each other for support and guidance to succeed.

The best form of recovery for individuals with a mental health diagnosis is providing others with empathy and reaching out to the clients from an equal perspective. Understanding that everyone has their flaws and the stigma should be taken away can really make a positive impact on your life. The community and society have to become more aware of the perspectives that exist in the lives of the ones that are impacted by mental health. As a result, it is up to the client and individuals with a mental health diagnosis to use their voice and try to enhance their goals so that they can be successful and find self-acceptance.

Active Minds. Org

There are many mental health organizations that are aiming to help individuals faced with a mental health condition. NAMI is a mental health organization that is there to help you care for your mental health condition. There are programs that are also helpful for families. The Active Minds organization was created by Alison Malmon who had the desire to help destigmatize mental health conditions after her brother committed suicide. This organization is meant for students as they are trying to find their way in life when faced with a mental health condition.

This organization helps give you some feedback and extra information about what mental health is all about and how it can make a tremendous impact on society. The organization is now established in Washington, D.C. There are a lot of programs that are used to help combat the illnesses that exist along with educating society so that others can be more informed. Understanding your mental health diagnosis is hard and I find myself trying to do the best I can to focus on being the best person I can be.

Active Minds provides you with insight and statistics about mental health that justifies why mental health is such an important topic to discuss about. This is a great organization that has made a tremendous impact on the lives of thousands.

Reference: Activeminds.org

Jed Campus.Org

In my experience while at Western Washington University, I found that there was a lot of help from the mental health counselors and the disability services center. There were times when I didn't know where to go and how to start with my studies. As a result, I found myself finding help from the disability services center where I could find help. This help looked like extra time allocation for tests and tutoring options. Although I did not end up graduating from Western, I still found that being given the ability to see a counselor every week is empowering and liberating as I don't feel tied down to the stress that can be a big result of the rigorous coursework in college.

While I was at Bellingham Technical College, the disability office was helping students become successful academically. When it comes to the counseling services, I know they were always there to support me in my academic endeavors and wanted to see me succeed. There is absolutely nothing wrong with seeing a counselor. In fact, just like the LMHC mentioned earlier in the book, "Everyone can benefit from counseling" (LMHC). There is so much support out there and you just need to be willing to take the first step in your life that will be best for you. Don't give in to the stigma that asking for help from others is a bad thing. I have been the most successful when I know that I had support on my back as I could fall back upon something. With that being said, you really need the pound inside of your chest to achieve your wildest dreams and goals.

There is so much that you need to do to stay on top of your goals. Self advocating when you have a mental health diagnosis is something that you can do to stay on top of your life. Pursuing your truth in life and focusing on your needs is the most vital thing that you can do to give your life purpose and meaning. Believing in yourself comes prior to self advocating. The action of using your voice when times get tough is what makes you or breaks you when considering the direction that your life is heading. It is simple with what you do to create self-advocacy: use your voice. You have a voice and you can tell others what you need to do to engage in routines that will propel you to success.

When I got out of the hospital, I had to rely on the mental health professionals to help me walk through my recovery. I had to learn that my voice is powerful.

My self-advocacy at times looked like walking into the hospital and getting "stuck" in the mental health ward for a month at a time where I had to learn how to manage my symptoms of bipolar. Self-advocacy is something that can take years to develop. You go through the struggles and find your way on top again is what you can do to climb the ladder of success.

What is your way of expressing yourself to the world and showing to yourself that you have the potential to find your own passion?

Earning your own income to support yourself is what self-advocacy looks like when you are trying to comeback 2 success. Even if it means starting part time, there are times when it doesn't feel like enough. Giving yourself grace to embrace the journey and do the best you can do at your workplace environment is what you can do to create connections and prove to yourself that you are capable of shooting for the stars.

You must lose yourself before you can learn to find yourself again. Along this journey you will find your voice and can focus on continuing to improve yourself. I found myself having to go through the struggles and difficulties in life to find myself and my passion. The tears and all the struggle are what builds you up and makes you a stronger human being. The connection with self-advocacy is where you will find your passion if you continue to keep going and try your best to give it your all everyday like it was your last.

I wanted to give up when I got out of the hospital. I felt like there was nobody who could relate to the troubles that came my way with being bipolar and focusing on my recovery.

You are your best advocate for your dreams and goals. What you say and talk about on the daily is what will become of you and can reap the rewards if you keep working on yourself, your passion and aiming for the stars. There will be people that try to get inside your head and break you down. This is a part of life and you have the choice to believe them or decide that you can persevere and find your voice to aim for that will help you overcome the negativity.

8. Passion pathfinding: From retail to Motivational speaking

I have had a lucrative work background in the grocery industry, automotive sales industry, pharmaceutical manufacturing business, landscaping and fast-food industry. All these jobs tested my skills and gave me a lot of experience. The point I am trying to make is that you have a lot to learn about yourself and to figure out what works best for your life. This great nation offers a lot of accommodations for individuals with disabilities or mental illnesses. There is absolutely nothing stopping you from pursuing your dreams or a job that seems to be a good fit for you. Hard work is the answer when trying to find your potential and it can have a big impact on your happiness.

I want to go more in depth regarding the different jobs that I worked and what I learned from each of them. To start with, my first job at Haggen grocery store was essential. I was a 17-year-old with a goal: save $5,000 dollars to pay for my first car. I started at Haggen as a courtesy clerk cleaning restrooms, bagging groceries and pushing carts. This was incredibly rewarding because I was earning income for my goal. I found myself working on the weekends and some days during the week. I was in high school and playing sports, so I had to learn good time management skills. This is a skill that can be acquired and positively impact your life. The time management skills that I learned were very helpful as I found myself balancing a lot of work on my plate. This has had a long-lasting impact on my life as I have continued to balance work, school and other ambitions.

Flashfowrard to 2019, I decided that I wanted to start planning a move to a major city in the U.S. Two major cities that I had my eyes set on were Los Angeles, California and Seattle, Washington. While I was at work, I found myself doing a lot of heavy research that would help make the move possible. The most useful source that I found effective was craigslist. This website was very helpful for finding a place to live. In fact, this was how I found my first and second place to live in Seattle. I used Roomies.com to find my first place in Cerritos, California.

For those of you with a mental illness, it is still possible to move away from home and into a major city like Seattle or LA. You just have to want it bad enough and dedicate time to make it happen. The fears and failures that you come across will be so rewarding because you know that you are trying your best.

Preparation is key to make such a move possible. This looks like getting your finances in order. When I moved to Seattle, I had over $7,000 saved up so that I could pay for my rent for a couple months and have a safety net. Rent was $985/month including utilities for the first 6 months. Living in Seattle is not cheap. Also, I had a job lined up and ready to go once I arrived.

Having backups and proper support will get you to where you want to go. Solid steps will help guide you into being the best you can be and help you strive for a life that is fulfilling while in a city. Another important thing to think about are the positives and negatives to living in the city.

I lived in Seattle for over 9 months and Southern California for over 6 months. I have learned a lot about how to be happy and healthy while living with a mental illness. All the growing struggles and difficulties turned me into a stronger person and the rewards have been so worth the strides to earn success.

Ever since the age of 17,I have been mostly working in the retail-grocery industry. This has had a transformative effect on my life as I have found myself growing tremendously. I have been able to work well with both coworkers and customers. This helped me to get out of my comfort zone through socializing with customers and coworkers daily.

Furthermore, while living in Seattle, I was around a lot of different people who challenged my perspectives and enriched my experience and added more value to my life. The city life is like none other. People are fast paced with their life and interested in how you are going to further pursue your dreams.

The drawback to city life is there are a lot of people that could take advantage of you. Vulnerability is important only to an extent. What I mean by this is that finding the balance of knowing when to say something and when to say nothing at all is helpful in anyone's personal development. I say this because this has helped me in my journey thus far. Furthermore, if you are far away from home, it can be hard to find friends and you can get lonely. There were times when I felt lonely because I was working so much and didn't have anyone to relate to and try to feel happy about the goals that I have set for myself.

City life isn't for everyone. Picking a city to live in is like going on an adventure (like many things in life). Unless you try and do some research, you will never know what the best fit for you and your career aspirations is. For example, if you wanted to be a country music singer, Nashville, Tennessee would be the best fit for you. Also, if you wanted to be an actor, then Los Angeles, California or Vancouver, B.C. would be a great fit. I want to be an entrepreneur, writer and motivational speaker so I choose Seattle and Southern California to best fit my goals and dreams. Your dreams are yours and only you get to decide how you want to live your life and where you live. The city life is something that can add a lot of value to your life and can enrich it tremendously.

Sometimes the ideal job opportunity doesn't come for a while. If this is the case, it is better to start somewhere rather than nowhere. When you don't have the luxury to pick and choose, self-advocacy can help you discover enjoyment at your work.

To recap, a job can help you grow and it is beneficial to find the right long term career that fits your lifestyle, passion and mental health. You deserve that for yourself period. There are jobs that exist that will help satisfy your mental health needs and happiness. I recommend reaching out to your mental health professional or case manager to help brainstorm some ideas about your ideal career path. Don't let your mental illness or disability get you down and prevent you from pursuing your passion.

When you are faced with a mental health condition, life can be hard. Due to these circumstances, it is essential that you focus on the positive steps that you are taking towards your goals and dreams. It can be immensely hard to do this and I find that at times I don't want to do anything and just give up. This is the negativity that we all have inside of us.

Taking action over complacency creates results that are priceless in a transformative way. There is true beauty to be found in getting back up and choosing to stand up for what you want by putting in the work. Taking action is what you need to do every single day in order to find authentic success.

You have to be willing to take risks, put yourself out there and expect failure. Yet in the midst of it all, you should also recognize that the journey of what you learn is part of the growth that is so authentic to your life. When you start to realize that mistakes and failures come with success, life gets a whole lot better. To put into a few words, without failure, success isn't possible. Facing each problem with an attitude of optimism and positivity will get you further than you think. People will start to recognize your abilities and dedication.

Choosing to focus on yourself and wellbeing is the best starting point that can give you insight and control for how you can go and get what you are destined for.

You are the only person that has the power to make change in your life. Taking action is the hardest step to take and will have a big impact on the trajectory of your life. Going against the grain and what society tells you that you should or shouldn't do will help you to make a lasting impact in the mental health community and beyond. I aim to be a better person than I was yesterday and to do something that will have lasting effects in the sense that others can learn from the ups and downs that I have experienced while having Bipolar Disorder.

Waiting for tomorrow to make a change will result in little to no progress on what the things are in life that really matter the most. Taking action is what you need to do everyday in order to make your wildest dreams manifest itself.

Finally, have fun with it and don't give up when things aren't going so well. When I quit my job at Haggen, things seemed to be getting progressively worse and, eventually, I ended up back in the hospital. Things got worse because I made it that way and didn't reach out for help when I really needed it. Therefore, take action even when it is the hard thing to do. Don't let others judge you for the actions that you take to try and overcome your problems. You are wise in recognizing that action needs to be taken in order to focus on living a happy and healthy life.

Finding your passion when you are faced with a mental illness is something that has taken me years. I had to go through the struggles that came along with being diagnosed. All the hospitalizations and the fears of being the way that I am just led to feelings of negativity, doubt and depression. Being an individual that can move forward regardless of the circumstances you are faced with creates a lot of resiliency and character.

When it comes to following your passion and finding it in the midst of the trouble, look into the stars and realize that you are someone that is special and who has a lot of gifts which can help to make this world a better place. You get to choose how you want to live a life that is enriching and rewarding. Fulfillment comes when you commit to yourself and open your eyes to the beauty of life that unveils itself with the struggle. The pain will soon pass and you will learn to develop a thick skin which will help you to become a more resilient person.

Finding your passion takes time and there are so many ways to find it. The best way is to try something new that pushes you outside of your comfort zone. When you are faced with fear and don't think you are good enough, that struggle can help fuel your success. Don't give in to the doubt, fear and other emotions that are dragging you down and pinning you up against the wall. Learning how to get back up on your own two feet is a beautiful thing of life.

At the end of the day, life is a solo path that only you can decide what you want. Finding your passion takes work and sacrifice. There are apps like Meetup where you can find a group of people in your city that have a lot of different interests. Learning something new and trying to grow as a person can have a lot of positive outcomes, if you are willing to apply yourself. For starters, it could look like showing up once a week to participate in a soccer league. After some time, you can learn something about yourself and see if your new hobby is something that you are actually interested in.

A life well lived is one in which you are living out your passion and that said passion is helping you earn an income. After you push yourself to your greatest potential, you can see results start to emerge. When your work or passion doesn't seem like work, you have reached a new level of personal development. Many successful people realize this and choose to put their discomfort into their work and help make an impact to share their story. Money is a byproduct of hard work, dedication and commitment.

Finally, you get what you put into it. A key component of life is to do the best you can at everything that you do. When you give things your best effort, you'll get better results. As a result, a better life that will help you find happiness and fulfillment. Don't stop reaching for the stars. There will be people in your life that come across you for some time in your life and don't think you can reach what you have painted in your mind. Prove it to yourself that your passion is truly possible and that you can overcome the doubters. Finding your passion is not possible without accepting failure. If you are willing to accept failure, the process can become easier and easier until your goal is achieved. Only you know what you can accomplish. Nobody else can define you or tell you what you can and can't do.

I have always been a driven person. Even as a child, I told my grandma I wanted to be rich. So, what I ended up doing, was collecting aluminum cans and saving them up for money. I remember going to the recycling station with my grandma where we would watch the cans get weighed. Then, we would watch the cans go onto the conveyor belt and get crushed. This taught me discipline as I reached out to family members and started to collect cans until the money started to "stack" up.

My drive and passion for success all started with a sibling rivalry between me and my cousin Clark. Clark is a 6'2" quarterback who has played all throughout his life both domestically and internationally. We have always been close and very competitive with each other. We would find ourselves fighting to be the best and over who won first place in a race. It was like life was a race against each other and all that mattered was getting the first-place trophy. Later, I learned that it is a race against yourself and how you as a person are responsible for your actions that creates what you want in life.

While we were traveling and living in Central America, Clark and I would find ourselves fighting to be the first to finish dinner, fighting to win a wrestling match and even on the soccer field. Sports helped me fuel my passion for success as I was able to be more focused on one thing and doing everything I could to be the best at that one thing. The sports that I played helped me tremendously grow and personally develop.

There were times when I felt like giving up but I got through it using my inner drive and passion.

Knowing and understanding that I was in the driver's seat of my life and that I got to write my own destiny was very enticing. And guess what, you can do it too!

My hustler spirit has helped me turn my life into a man that is hungry for success. There have been times when I don't always see the positives in life because the world has been so unkind to me. The fact is that the world can be unkind to all of us and if we don't find our inner spirit and drive to succeed, we will never find our truest potential.

I have learned that failure doesn't define me. It is how we learn to stand up on our own two feet and continue to persevere. Life is what you make it and I firmly believe that we all have a purpose that is beyond us. Finally, your spirit is what helps keep you on pace to accomplish your dreams.

Keep your spirit alive and let it shine to the world. This is because there are many people out there who want to see you succeed and who want your true colors to shine. If you are focused and hungry for success, you will become that and embody that mindset. Your spirit is the fire that is waiting to shine and light up the whole world. We all have a spirit inside of us. Some of us choose to let it shine bright for the rest of our lives, while others keep the spirit hidden. I am here to say that showing your true colors is not always the easiest part about life. There will be times when you are faced with decisions to make regarding how to react to the circumstances life throws at you. I want to encourage you to continue to stay strong and stand up for what you believe in. The world is counting on you. Your own potential is waiting for your light to shine.

Your mindset is one of the most powerful things that you can control, even when the inevitable trials and tribulations of life come your way. Your mindset is the mast of a boat in a stormy ocean. Keep it that way and rely on it when all else fails. There will be times when you are struggling to find hope, peace, joy and love. Don't look down. Keep your head up and keep pushing on because you know that deep down inside there is a fire that you are waiting to show the world.

I often find myself thinking about the struggles I have had to overcome and how I often tried to overcome them in my life. As I continue to get older, I am starting to learn that we can't control everything in our lives. The number one thing that we can do is to rely on ourselves to react to the situations that life brings us. I firmly believe that regardless of your mental health diagnosis, that there is nothing getting in the way of you finding your own passion and going out and making it happen.

My life has dramatically changed ever since I started to believe that I could do something big. I can do something great, powerful and can change the world. What I am trying to say is that if you don't have the desire to succeed and the passion to fuel you as you go along the way, you will never reach your highest potential. Don't listen to the haters who say that you can't do something. You get to choose how you respond to the situations that come your way in life.

The fuel for your passion consists of a hearty meal and can end with confidence to post that new video of your goals on social media. You can be an inspiration for so many people if you believe it. I remember that when I was 19, I had the desire to be a leader and influential person that would change the world. I told this to my uncle at age 19 before I ended up going through hell and back. The only difference is that I can make an impact on life every day. Every day that we wake up and contribute to society and impact others can make a difference.

Some examples of fueling your passion are going for a run or doing something athletic. Trying something new is another way to explore your interests and find your passion.

To put it bluntly, there is absolutely no excuse for you to not be focused on your passion every day. If you want it bad enough, you will make it happen. Just thinking about it and making decisions that will dictate the further development of your passion is where you can see the results come to life. There is so much more that you can do around personally developing yourself and your dreams. You need to have the stability and desire to succeed. If you don't have an interest in succeeding or aren't able to accept the troubles that will come your way along the road, you will not succeed. There will be times when you will want to quit.

I am learning that it is okay to not have all the answers right away. Let the pain fuel your passion. After I was done crying in the hospital, I learned that it is important to rely on the mental health professionals for guidance and their professional recommendations to help me stay grounded. If you aren't focused on your goals and dreams, complacency can creep into your life. For example, I was too focused on telling the world that I was "okay" when I was in need of help and someone to help guide me through my challenges. The desire to win and to find passion is necessary in order to find happiness and the person that you are born on this earth to be.

When I was in the mental health system, I saw time and time again that some people were too afraid to put in the work to improve themselves and gain control of their lives.

Finally, you are your best advocate at work. There will be days when you just want to stay in bed at home. It is a matter of finding the strength and motivation to be better than you were yesterday. If you can tell yourself that you are gaining momentum and progress for your life and mental health, more power to you. Finding enjoyment within your work is what you will need to get you to where you want to go and earn an income that is well lived for.

Seattle is a place where you can chase big dreams. I am a small town boy with big town dreams. For this reason, living in Bellingham, WA limits my opportunities for growth that I can find from within. This is the reason why I chose Seattle over other major cities. Not long after, I moved to Southern California because I wanted to continue to grow.

I hope that my story will encourage and inspire you to chase your passion regardless of your circumstances so that you can be happy and healthy.

9. Conclusion: Success over Stigma

The actor Will Smith once said, "to build a wall you must lay one brick at a time as perfectly as possible. Once you've laid one brick, focus on the next and lay it as perfectly as possible. So on and so forth until you have a wall." By focusing on this you can avoid making seductive, fun, easy impulsive decisions.

The hard choice is to sacrifice the easy route and focus on what you can do to engage in choices that are fruitful for your success. Also, learning to develop self-control will help you become more mentally successful as you learn to control your actions and to make calculated choices, resulting in success.

Learning to take calculated risks is developed through failure. Once you start learning how to fail and get back up on your feet, things get easier and you can start to get into a rhythm of finding your own balance and level of stability needed to focus on a healthy lifestyle. Your mental health is your foundation for self-control. Practicing calculated risks will get you to where you want to go and can be a major contributor towards the success that you are so hoping to obtain.

As hard as it is to not run away from yourself and your diagnosis, you can't run away from who you are. You will always be the person that you were born to be until the day you die. Love yourself. Simple as that.

There have been times when I couldn't find a single reason to love myself. My faith in God and family was what I had to lift me up. Running away from your diagnosis or problems only solves the problem temporarily. If you choose to run from your problems for your whole life, you won't last. There are times when we want to feel accepted and loved. Going through the pain and reaching out for help can aid you in overcoming the obstacles associated with a mental health struggle or diagnosis.

I want to challenge you to understand that nothing and nobody but yourself is stopping you from going out and pursuing your passion. Running away from your problems is just like shooting yourself in the foot. I ran so many times to the point that I ended up in the hospital. I was foolish to think that I had all the answers to my problems. It was once I went through the struggles and had to learn how to keep going despite the challenges that I learned that I didn't have to run away from anything.

I want to bring up overcoming stigma and how this plays a pivotal role in the lives for those who are struggling with a mental health diagnosis or mental illness. If you were to ask me if I would be the man that I am today without my diagnosis, I would tell you absolutely no way. However, now I am an entrepreneur, author and keynote speaker who won't let anyone get in my way. With that being said, overcoming stigma starts from within. Society treats you differently because there are symptoms and side effects that come with the diagnosis.

It is vital that you choose to stand up on your own two feet and recognize that you are special and one of a kind. Don't let a mental health diagnosis like Bipolar disorder or schizophrenia or depression tear you down and prevent you from pursuing what you want to do and love.

Self love can help guide you in times of trouble. Don't give up, even when things are getting rough. Even I feel like giving up sometimes. My will to succeed is greater than anything else. There is nobody else who has the responsibility to continue to persevere through all the adversity that life throws at me and you. Know your worth and continue to recognize this when others doubt you and test you.

Finding your true passion and desire to succeed despite your diagnosis can be hard. When you dedicate yourself to an idea or topic, this will help guide your spirit to getting to where you want to go in the future. Mental health recovery can be hard to accomplish and sustain. Without support from others, it will be difficult to get out of the depressive state. Don't give up when your mental health challenges are hard to overcome. Talking with a counselor can be very hard to do because trusting someone you don't know can be hard to adjust and open up to. When you don't have the sense of being heard for who you are and what you are feeling, life can be more difficult than it needs to be. Your success is reliant upon your ability to stand up for what you believe in and your ability to push yourself out of your comfort zone.

I decided to see a counselor but still felt incomplete. This is the reality for many people. The pressure of my family who was trying to help was hard to handle. I needed to recognize from within that there was something that needed to be changed.

Another valuable lesson that I am learning is when you give all you've got, good things start to come your way. I want to emphasize the importance of giving. Sacrifice will help you accomplish your dreams along the way towards your destiny. Let this book be a guide to overcoming your obstacles and focusing on how to succeed and find your true passion. Not having a passion, it is like a flower unable to photosynthesize to its potential. Now wouldn't that be sad, to be the flower that didn't grow because you didn't put enough energy into yourself? It is also important to determine where you choose to plant yourself. How you truly find the success and ability to grow towards your greatest potential is also from the environment that you surround yourself in. Don't let the next person push you around and tell you what and where they think you would be good at. Only YOU know what and where that spark is inside of you.

The best way to find the spark is to try something new. I have found success when I commit myself 100% to doing something and don't give up. Even when things get rough and I don't have all the answers, I continue to push on. When the results aren't what you had in mind, make changes and continue to move forward with a positive mindset.

Your opinion matters. You are valued and worth more than a million. You are rare and there is only one of you in the world. God made you in the way that he wanted you to be. God helps those who help themselves.

I have found that when times are tough it feels like the world is crashing down on my head, so I reach out to someone I trust and who understands me. Finding that one person and engaging in that relationship is important. When it seems like there is nobody around who understands you, you need to believe in yourself. Even when the odds are all against you. We all have the power to do so inside of us. Some choose to unlock it while others let it sit without any action. As time goes by with little to no action on parts of development of one's life, regret starts to creep in. Having been taken. Neglect hurts more than any discomfort you may face while trying to pursue your dreams.

So, create an action plan for yourself, start writing down your goals every day so that you can ensure success creating accountability in your goals and dreams. Your life is only as good as you make it. As I write this, I start to realize that the little things in life are what we value the most. Although most of us are in such a hurry to get rich and get to the top that we fail to recognize the beauty of what is right in front of us. So, for the next week or so, start to look for the small positives that happen in your everyday life.

When you are dealing with any type of mental health problem, there is stigma. Whether it be with depression, seeing a counselor, or being diagnosed with a mental illness, stigma exists. It is important to keep your head up and to surround yourself with people who are accepting of your diagnosis. The best way to promote change is to advocate for yourself and for what you need. Be a self-advocate and don't let the opinion of others get in the way of who you are and who you want to become.

Life is not a waiting game. You have to be a go-getter everyday and want your dream to come true to the point where you are working on it every day. Thinking about my goals, dreams and passion is something that I do everyday. I find myself craving success and if I don't get it, my heart will burst. There have been times when I didn't think that I could make it this far in my personal development and growth in my life. The move to Seattle and to Southern California has helped me find peace and happiness, face challenges and learn how to accept failure.

When I ask what is getting in the way of your life, the answer could be nothing. I want to break down the excuses and obligations that we all have. At the end of the day, we all only have 24 hours. It is how we use that time that makes all the difference. Your commitment to success is yours and yours only. You can reach for the stars. Your journey is authentic and different than anybody else's. The things that get in the way of my life are just excuses to not succeed.

As this book wraps up, I want to encourage you to view this book as life lessons and ideas to help you navigate through your ups and downs of life in your pursuit of happiness. My hope is that it will make you a better and more developed person to help you grow. There is so much life that I have lived and without the trials and tribulations, highs, lows, struggles and successes, I wouldn't be the person that I am today. I want the world to know that I will not judge your highs and lows. Various struggles and forms of oppression exist in this world that needs to change. The world is much better when there is harmony and peace. With the love and grace of god, I have been able to successfully navigate my life. In spite of the struggle of life, I found peace, love and joy.

My goal for you, as the reader, is to be inspired to create your own authentic story. The resources that I have listed in this book are meant to offer guidance and resources that will help you find the courage to overcome your mental health struggles.

My mental health struggles are currently manageable and they will not stop me from spreading my message that a boy with small dreams can still end up with a book that will inspire many. Nothing more than giving it your all everyday determines what you can and can't do. You are the captain of your boat. Set your boat in the direction of success and with the support of organizations like NAMI, therapists, doctors, family, friends and yourself you'll reach your destination. Like it says in the bible, "God helps those who help themselves" (Ephesians 2:4-10)

How has Bipolar changed my life? It has made me a stronger human being. I am now more aware of the mental health struggles that people deal with on a daily basis. It has given me perspective on how I can be of aid to those with similar struggles. Bipolar is very time demanding. I have found myself in discussion with other people who have similar struggles. Bipolar is just a mental illness and a mental illness is just a medical condition. It doesn't fully define me as a person.

I want to spread the word about the impact mental health is so important to everyone in life. The comeback 2 success that I made in my life is unique in its own way. You can comeback 2 success if you are willing to dedicate the time, work and effort. My desire to write this book came from the desire to make a difference in the world where I often felt like my life was neglected and basically forgotten. I felt like I was dead while in the hospital and was so lonely. I have found beauty in life through the pain and struggle that life brings our way. If you can find that in your own life, things start to get better and you will come to understand that pain is temporary. Noone is immune to it. You don't have to be reliant upon negative habits to numb the pain that comes with mental illness.

What I learned from struggling with bipolar is that you don't have to let it define you. It is only a part of you. When you accept that all you have control of is yourself and your choices, you can find freedom to grow and release yourself of the false sense of control over what life brings your way. We all are born alone and will die alone. All we have is ourselves for the rest of our life. As a result, it is imperative to learn how to love yourself and to give yourself grace to overcome the struggles headed your way. Your ability to succeed is dependent upon how you react to your circumstances and life experiences that you go through.

I had to respond to many different circumstances and I didn't know where to start. So many of us are just living to make it by. I had to go through hell and back multiple times before I learned that struggling made me who I am. The Bipolar Disorder diagnosis came as a result of my struggles. Receiving this diagnosis was out of my control. However, I still have control over how I react to the cards that I was dealt.

I learned that you are capable of achieving the things that you might doubt. Doubt is a feeling that has blinded so many of us. Once we hit a wall, we seem to retreat and run back to our comfort zone. Getting over depression or any other type of mental illness takes work, courage and a whole lot of faith in yourself to get over the negative times when it felt like there was no hope in life. As I reflect on the past 5 years of my life, I have found that you are the one who creates your own path. Friends come and go like the seasons but family remains with you. There is nobody more important in your life than God and it is important to believe that he will help you find strength to live your best life. I have found that the biggest lesson that can be found in life is based on the learning of your life failures.

It is my optimism that has led me to be content with what I have. Times when I would have to eat alone or be away from my family and friends, has taught me that you have to love yourself before you can love another human being. Humans are meant to be social and if you are able to make a connection with both yourself and somebody else, you are winning.

Going through the process of overcoming obstacles and trusting in myself has gotten me far. In life, we are faced with many struggles that make us who we are. There is so much to be grateful for. This includes my move to Seattle and California which was a demonstration of faith and commitment in myself.

We all walk different paths in life. I firmly believe that the stages of life that I have passed through and explored here can act as a lesson to others on how to navigate through life with bipolar disorder or other mental health struggle and how to find a way to be successful and crush your goals.

What I went through and had to overcome has made me a stronger human being. You are wise if you choose to learn from your mistakes and take risks for what can make a difference in your life along with others.

Your life is something special and it is irreplaceable. Once you start to realize that you have the potential to do whatever you set your mind to, you will realize that things can get better. Make a better life for yourself and set an example for others. Encourage them to chase their dreams. All the pain that I have gone through to get to where I am today is priceless. You have your gifts just like I have mine.

You want to be successful? You have to have the vision. I remember walking to Whatcom Community College, taking the bus, realizing that I have the potential to do big things. Listening to G-Eazy's "Me, Myself, and I" I realized that I have to prove to myself that I can do something big. I mean something that will be worth living life. Something that is my passion.

Questions for Discussion:

1.   What is your problem that you are facing with mental health?

2.   How are you focusing on taking steps to comeback 2 success?

3.   Who is your best source of help?

4.   How are you searching for your answers to be more aware about yourself and your mental health struggles?

5.   When are you deciding to take a risk that might help you get in the right direction for your life?

6.   What do you need to do RIGHT NOW to take ACTION for your benefit?

My hope is that you will find something of substance that will lift you out of whatever stage of life you are in and can offer hope when it seems like there is none. When I didn't feel like there was anything going my way, it was music that helped me sustain myself and encouraged me to continue on my journey. Regardless of a mental illness, it is a matter of dealing with the real highs and lows of life that are true for everyone. I have enjoyed being able to share my story with those who are interested in hearing the story of an "average" small town boy who didn't give up on his big town dreams.

Stay Blessed and Stay Strong!

Yours truly,

Brandon Burbank

Official Notes from Interviews:

Interview With Rich Notes:

Interview Q&A With Rich Kurtzman, MA, Spanish Applied Linguistics and Second Language Acquisition:

1. What is your educational background? Can you tell us a little bit about your work related expertise?

Studied Spanish and Russian in Undergrad and a little bit of Business and Psychology.

Studied Abroad in St.Petersburg, Russia.

Studied Abroad 1 Semester in Madrid, Spain.

Masters Degree in Spanish Applied Linguistics and Second Language Acquisition

Worked for Study Abroad Organization in U.S.A. where he was recruiting.

Taught Spanish, Intercultural Communication, Internships and worked in various cultural and academic side in Barcelona

Started Barcelona SAE in 2009. Founder and CEO.

Led high school students abroad, Internship in Milan, Italy with a study abroad program

2. What are some of the ways you want the study abroad programs globally become more accessible for students with disabilities?

TODOS - The Outcomes Based Diversity Outreach Strategy. Increasing Inclusivity in study abroad and trying to help more underrepresented students go abroad and increase the training for them as well as staff, homestay families.

3. How can study abroad programs accommodate better for providing students with disabilities with an opportunity to study abroad successfully?

Letting them know that it is possible. There are resources that can help provide for you. There will be resources that can help your university. For Barcelona, mobility is the best and public transportation with more lines that are there for support. Logistically, housing is something to keep in mind. Continuous follow up and support.

4. What are your hopes as you look forward to becoming a more accessible study abroad program?

More students have the opportunity to study abroad and have a memorable experience like myself when I studied abroad in Barcelona, Spain. Having a role model to help lead a path for future study abroad students who are interested.Take the leap of faith!

5. What can study abroad programs improve upon with their support for students who faced culture shock? Reverse culture shock?

Preparation is the key. It is helpful for study abroad programs to have pre departure programs to help create more...

And guided reflection by experts in the program to discuss what students are going through and see things from a different perspective.

Especially to be more accessible to all students, this has to come in different formats: written, verbal, conversation.

6. What is the best advice you can give to a student with a disability who is considering studying abroad?

Talk to somebody else who has done it. Might have a similar disability. Be as prepared as you can by talking to professionals. Make sure it is the right thing.

It is not the right thing for everyone. Maintain support networks from a distance.

Be prepared to not be prepared for everything.

Brandon: Be optimistic and follow your heart. Your instincts are attracting you to what you want to become a reality.

7. What are some big problems that the study abroad programs are still facing related to mental health and disabilities?

The number of students with disabilities are growing very quickly. More instances of anxiety and depression. Just means that we as a study abroad program need to be more prepared. Not everyone is a licensed doctor and understands the medication. Resources for professional help would be of great benefit.

Being prepared for the increase of students studying abroad with disabilities

8. Anything else you would like to share?

We have had some incredible and inspiring students in the past who have been in wheelchairs, deaf, with cerebral palsy, mobility challenges, mental health issues, and all sorts and I am so proud of them for taking the challenge to come abroad, when it is challenging for anyone to begin with, but with extra challenges, it's that much harder. Some of my best memories are working with the students who "gave us more work" logistically but the reward is priceless.

Amber Geer Interview:

Tell us a little bit about yourself...

28 years old. Go to Northwest University Online Program. Soccer is my passion. Bachelor's degree from Seattle Pacific University 2018 Bachelors of Arts in Psychology

What have you learned about the mental health industry since enrolling in your classes to become a counselor?

Since enrolling into the graduate program at Northwest University

Everyone shows symptology, can lead to underdiagnosis and misdiagnosis.

Abnormal Psychology, eye opening class

Biological, DNA/genetic predisposition to mental health/illness

Nurtured: the environment you grew up in and how that impacts your ability to process emotions, engage, be in relation with people, etc. "ATTACHMENT THEORY"

What are the most important topics or ways of thinking that need to be discussed for students pursuing a career in mental health?

> a.   Ways of thinking: open minded, critical thinking skills,
>
> b.   Genuineness, self reflection; being aware of potential <u>transference and counter transference</u>

How can the mental health industry be changed in a positive way to better develop care and recovery for those affected by mental illness?

Access and advocacy are the biggest challenges that this nation is facing.

How can the schools better teach students about mental health?

Teachers need to be aware and educated about mental health. Open to the concept and have a basic understanding of what to do when a child says to you "I am feeling sad..."

What needs to change in the nation to help people overcome their addictions, depression and other mental illnesses?

Better access and insurance needs to be less restrictive for giving out diagnosis and longer time to see the therapist or mental health professionals.

You mentioned that you are going to school for counseling... How can counseling add value to someone who is struggling with their mental health?

Added support to the client's support system. There are some clients who come in with no support system. Counseling is part of the management of your symptoms. Counseling is not for everybody. What works best for you and your life. **Finding what works best for you and your mental illness.**

Interview Questions for Dr. Jantz

Brandon Burbank

5/1/2020

1. Dr. Jantz, what has been your biggest accomplishment throughout your career in mental health?

2. Educational background: doctorate in counseling and psychology

Growth of the Center A Place of Hope. International influence in the area of whole person care

3. What are some of the biggest issues that are still needing to be solved in the mental health industry? Due to the pandemic, depression and anxiety. WHO (World Health Organization) says that depression is a worldwide problem

4. For those in higher education, what is the best piece of advice you could give students to help achieve results that will be long lasting for achieving mental health goals?

A lot of opportunities in the field of mental health. Be encouraged about the future opportunity. You are needed.

For those that are trying to comeback 2 success, what advice can you give to someone who was faced with a mental illness or health condition?

Recovery is always possible and with all of our pain comes great opportunity. Opportunity to change other peoples life.

6. How can this nation make strides to eradicate stigma around mental health?

Addiction field, first there was a lot of shame. Now it is okay to talk about shame. They are talking about getting help. Encouraging to get the word out that it is okay to ask for help.

7. For those that are pursuing med school or any type of higher education, what can students do to make a positive change as they gain more knowledge, experience and expertise in the mental health industry?

Themes through the book "Healing Depression For Life" . Great opportunity to spread the words of hope.

"Plan for people's wellness" by asking for help and getting good care we can help encourage.

Questions for Matt:

What is your mental health diagnosis?

Bipolar 1 disorder

When did this occur?

First experienced symptoms in 6th grade. 11 or 12 years old. First diagnosed at 14 years old.

How has it impacted your life?

Manifested itself as a struggle in the early years. Has been something that I can't ignore but I have always strived to live with it and be successful.

What is the main objective that you are doing to maintain a happy and healthy lifestyle?

Taking my meds as prescribed. Attending medical appointments. Living a clean life.

What advice would you give to someone who has recently been struggling with mental health and are trying to comeback 2 success?

Reach out for help if you haven't already. You can do this. There is hope.

Any other thoughts you might have that you would like to share with the reader?

Many people who are successful and or famous as well as your everyday person have lived with and overcome this life struggle as well. You can do this. Take it a step at a time. You are loved by at least some family and friends. Try to acknowledge the love and support that you have in your life.

How do you learn to overcome the stigma that exists in mental health?

I try to not take everything so personally, especially when it comes to judgement and mistreatment. And neglect. Opening up to others who may have been going through the same things as you. Not forgetting that you have a voice.

Interviewee: Zack

Date:

Time:

B: Zack, could you tell us a little bit about yourself? What is your educational background?

Z: I received my bachelor's degree in psychology and my master's degree in clinical mental health counseling. I completed my 3 years of required post-graduation supervision in 2018 and subsequently became fully licensed in Georgia as a LPC (licensed professional counselor).

B: What impact does mental health programs like Skyland trail have on someone dealing with a mental illness?

Z: I feel like there are many considerations to take into account when considering how impactful, either positive or negative, a mental health program, like Skyland Trail can have. A few factors to consider would be: is the program an appropriate clinical fit for the mental illness in which you are struggling, is it a credible program that follows evidenced based practices, is the client ready and willing to fully participate in the program? If these factors are appropriately considered, then I believe a mental health program like Skyland Trail can have a tremendous positive impact in one's life. It has the potential to provide with the appropriate level of intensive care to help them better manage their mental illness.

B: What is the goal of Skyland trail when helping their client's comeback 2 success?

Z: I think this is best expressed by our mission, "Offering hope, changing lives." I feel our goal for every client seeking our services is to leave with a better understanding of themselves and their future goals and understanding that while their mental health diagnosis may play a role in that, it does not define who they are. We want every client to leave with the appropriate skills to manage their mental health and to feel confident in their ability to live a happy and successful life.

B: What is the best approach that a mental health organization can do to help their clients battling with a mental illness or mental health struggle?

Z: I believe that it starts and ends with compassion. Taking the time to understand them as a whole person, and not just their mental illness, is key. Then using that information to treat the whole person psychologically, medically, nutritionally and psychically. This is something I believe Skyland Trail does exceptionally well.

B: How can society learn to grow and move forward to be more accepting for individuals with a mental illness?

Z: I believe that it all starts with building awareness through education and training. People are always going to fear the things they do not fully understand, so with more funding to provide education and trainings, we would be able to start moving in the right direction.

B: What value does Skyland trail enrich in someone's life if they attended a place like a mental health program?

Z: I believe that Skyland Trail believes in ultimately helping clients identify their values and then helping them better cultivate them in their daily lives. In my experience, one value that run through all of the work we do is self-love. We want to help people not only accept themselves, but to love themselves and recognize how their gifts positively impact their world and those around them.

B: How have you and Skyland trail grown since its first opening back in 1989?

Z: Skyland Trail has been in operation for over 30 years. Over the years it has grown to span multiple campuses, recently expanding to include adolescents aged 14-17, and offer evidenced based treatment to both adults and adolescents with complex psychiatric diagnoses. Personally, I attribute so much of what I have learned about mental health and effective forms of treatment to my time at Skyland Trail. Working at Skyland Trail has helped me grow not only as a clinician, but as a more well-rounded person. I am more confident in my abilities and cannot speak highly enough of the training and support I have received from them since I began working at Skyland in 2015.

B: As we look forward into the future, how can we as a community learn to grow and create more acceptance of others with a mental health diagnosis?

Z: This a great question, with many possible answers depending on whom you ask. I maintain that building awareness through education and trainings is going to be the best increase people's knowledge of mental health. With education, comes understanding and with understanding, the hope would be that acceptance would follow. I think there have been efforts made, and there is much more that needs to be done. It will not be an easy task and it will mean getting support from community and government leaders at varying levels of influence.

Works Cited:

Janes, Beth. *Why It's Important to Schedule More Downtime for Your Brain*. Shape,

www.shape.com/lifestyle/mind-and-body/why-its-important-schedule-more-downtime-your-

brain.

NAMI website. NAMI, 2019, nami.zendesk.com/hc/en-us/articles/360025157333-What-does-NAMI-do-and-what-is-its-mission-.

DNEWS , 12 Dec. 2012, www.seeker.com/an-illustrated-history-of-the-mental-asylum-1766218599.html.

Clear, James. *Summary of Atomic Habits: An Easy and Proven Way to Build Good Habits and Break Bad Ones*. Summary ed., GO Books, 2018, pp. 68-89.

Mental Health Overview. Web MD, p. 1, www.webmd.com/mental-health/default.htm.Fusco, DOMINIC J. *Statistics to Overturn Every Fear About Studying Abroad*. GoAbraod, 2017, www.goabroad.com/articles/study-abroad/statistics-about-study-abroad.

Janes, Beth. *Why It's Important to Schedule More Downtime for Your Brain*. Shape,

www.shape.com/lifestyle/mind-and-body/why-its-important-schedule-more-downtime-your-

Brain.

Jay, Meg. *The Defining Decade: Why Your Twenties Matter And How to Make the Most of Them Now*. Grand Central Publishing, 2013.

Mental Health Counselor, Licensed. Personal interview. 17 Mar. 2020.

Personal Interview with Amber Geer, BA

Personal Interview with Zack Garner, MA

Personal Interview with Amy Armstrong, BA

Personal Interview with Matt McGaha

Personal Interview with Dr. Gregory Jantz, Phd.

Personal Interview with Rich Kurtzman, MA